CULTURAL TOURISM

Tourism at World Heritage Sites: The Site Manager's Handbook

The ICOMOS International Committee on Cultural Tourism

Second Edition

This revised and illustrated edition was made possible through a grant from the American Express Foundation, and produced by US/ICOMOS in cooperation with the World Tourism Organization.

The volume was first produced by US/ICOMOS, the Secretariat of the ICOMOS International Committee on Cultural Tourism, with financial assistance from the National Park Service, U.S. Department of the Interior and the U.S. Department of State.

The work was published for the ICOMOS International Committee on Cultural Tourism in 1993 by the Sri Lankan National Committee of ICOMOS on the occasion of the 10th ICOMOS General Assembly in Colombo, Sri Lanka, 30 July - 4 August 1993, with the financial assistance of the Central Cultural Fund of the Government of Sri Lanka and UNESCO.

The second printing and distribution of the first edition were made possible in 1994 by a grant from the Montauk Foundation.

US/ICOMOS
401 F Street, NW Room 331
Washington, DC 20001-2728, USA
Tel: 202-842-1866; Fax: 202-842-1861; http://www.icomos.org/usicomos

ISBN: 92-844-0314-6

Published and distributed by the World Tourism Organization, Madrid Spain

Acknowledgements:

Editor: Donald Garfield
Cover Design: Eril Wiehahn
Book Design and Layout: Sheila Halstead

Foreword

The International Council on Monuments and Sites (ICOMOS) and the World Tourism Organization (WTO) are pleased to present this revised and expanded edition of *The Site Manager's Handbook.*

The Handbook was originally prepared by the US Committee of ICOMOS to mark the 10th General Assembly of ICOMOS, held in Colombo, Sri Lanka, in 1993. However, it proved its success by going out of print almost immediately.

Given the interest shown in heritage site management by its Environment Committee, WTO agreed to work with ICOMOS to produce a new, expanded version of the Handbook that could be distributed to a wider audience, including tourism officials as well as site managers.

With increasing media attention being paid to heritage sites and growing numbers of visitors being recorded at the best known venues, the subject of site management is today more topical than ever.

WTO and ICOMOS believe that organizations concerned with heritage have everything to gain by closer cooperation with those responsible for tourism. That is why the two institutions have joined forces to bring this essential reference to a worldwide readership.

Thanks are due to Ellen Delage, Programme Director for US-ICOMOS in Washington D.C., Peter Shackleford, former Chief of Environment at WTO and Deborah Luhrman, Chief of Communications at WTO for their contirbution to bringing this volume to print. The earlier edition was the work of Russell Keune.

Francesco Frangialli
WTO Secretary-General

Jean-Louis Luxen
ICOMOS Secretary-General

Preface to the First Edition

The ICOMOS International Specialized Committee on Cultural Tourism was organized in 1969. Arthur Haulot of Brussels, Belgium, a member of the Belgian National Committee of ICOMOS, was its founding chairman. In 1976 the committee prepared and adopted a charter which was later adopted at the 7th ICOMOS General Assembly meeting in 1984. The full text of this charter is reprinted in Appendix D, together with the full list of distinguished international institutions that helped in the preparation and in supporting its adoption.

For many years, Mr. Haulot led the ICOMOS tourism programs and represented the organization at numerous international meetings of tourism officials and conservation professionals. In 1986 the United States National Committee of ICOMOS agreed to accept the responsibility to serve as the Committee's secretariat. A reconstituted committee first met in 1987 during the 8th ICOMOS General Assembly in Washington, D.C. Mr. Haulot was appointed as an Honorary Member of the Committee.

At this 1987 meeting the ICOMOS Cultural Tourism Committee decided to review the terms of the Charter on Cultural Tourism to determine if it should be revised and up-dated. The committee also agreed that an improved bibliography of the field should be assembled. A newsletter would be issued and the committee sought to develop improved understanding of tourism issues by conservation leaders. It also agreed to reach out to commercial tourism leaders and associations to build closer ties to mutual advantage.

At the 9th ICOMOS General Assembly in Lausanne, Switzerland, in 1990, the committee received a sub-committee report that the charter should not be rewritten. The belief was that although much had changed, it was still a valid and valuable document. It was at this time that this handbook was envisioned, along with two others that were also prepared for this General Assembly. The other two handbooks were prepared by the ICOMOS International Specialized Committees on Conservation Economics and Archaeological Heritage Management. These three publications provide the basis of the General Assembly's scientific themes and discussions.

The 1990 publication, *Guidelines for the Management of World Cultural Heritage Sites*, edited by Sir Bernard Feilden and prepared under the sponsorship of International Centre for the Study of the Preservation and Restoration of Cultural Property (ICCROM) and UNESCO, deals with practice of site conservation and its related issues. This handbook on tourism is meant to be a companion volume. It is an expansion of Sir Berhard's Chapter 6, «The Visitors to World Cultural Sites.» Quite deliberately we have chosen to use committee members as authors and also to go outside of ICOMOS to involve travel industry leaders in the preparation and review of this handbook.

The primary audiences for this handbook are the individuals responsible for the administration of the cultural sites on the World Heritage List. The ICOMOS Committee on Cultural Tourism is proud to present this volume to ICOMOS members and to colleagues across the world interested in the protection and interpretation of World Heritage Sites.

Russell V. Keune, Vice President for Programs of US/ICOMOS and Secretary to the Committee, has coordinated the compilation, editing and production of this volume. We have tested his patience, depended on his knowledge and this volume is a product of his leadership. We are all grateful for his efforts and his friendship.

This handbook was also made possible by the volunteer work, written submissions and extensive financial and in-kind donations of material by:

- Management and corresponding members of the ICOMOS Cultural Tourism Committee; specifically, Graham Brooks (Australia), Lester Borley (UK), Peter Donovan (Australia), Jane

Fawcett (UK), Peter James (Australia), Russell V. Keune (USA), and Zeynep Aygen (Turkey).

- Individual members of US/ICOMOS who have generously contributed to the project based on their international experience with organizations such as the Organization of American States, UNESCO and the World Bank. We specially wish to recognize the substantial contributions of Gustavo Araoz, Jr., Hiroshi Daifuku and Edward Echeverria.

Its funding, editing, production and review distribution were made possible through the dedicated efforts of the Committee's Secretariat housed at US/ICOMOS in Washington, D.C. Particular thanks are due to Terry B. Morton, President; Ellen M. Delage, Program Officer; and Paul W. Hallam, Program Assistant.

The project was funded in part through a grant to US/ICOMOS for support of World Heritage Convention-related programs from the International Convention and Scientific Organizations Contributions, Office of International Organizations, U.S. Department of State, Washington, D.C., U.S.A.

Robertson E. Collins
Chairperson

Letter from American Express Foundation

The American Express Foundation is pleased to sponsor the revised edition of *Cultural Tourism at World Heritage Sites: The Site Manager's Handbook*, an important contribution to the safeguarding of the world's great tourism assets.

We recognize our vested interest in this handbook being as widely read and used as possible. The future of our company is linked to the future of the travel and tourism industry—the world's largest according to some. Travel and tourism now generates almost 11 percent of global Gross National Product and employs 262 million people worldwide—many of whose jobs are linked to travel to great historic sites. Study after study show that the chance to visit historic sites is one of the prime motivators of tourism and that heritage is often a key factor in a visitor's choice of one destination over another.

The economic argument for wise stewardship of these monuments is compelling. Just as important, they are a source of pride and identity for communities, regions, nations, and mankind. These are the reasons why we have so often collaborated in the past with ICOMOS, with UNESCO, and with private nonprofits such as World Monuments Fund to champion the cause of world heritage, and we are proud to continue to do so.

With the new edition of this handbook, we hope to assist the people most directly responsible for UNESCO World Heritage Sites in their sometimes conflicting responsibilities—not only to protect their sites but also make them hospitable to visitors. We believe that visitors to these sites who are well and thoughtfully received become part of a worldwide constituency to assure their survival so that they will be there for future generations to enjoy.

Mary Beth Salerno
President,
The American Express Foundation

Finding a Balance

World Heritage Sites include many of the planet's most outstanding attractions and grandest monuments of the past. For tourism promoters they act as magnets, while for the nation in which they are found they serve as icons that continue to influence current values. They are treasures in the fullest and deepest sense. They require management that preserves them for future generations and, at the same time, makes them accessible to the public for purposes of education and enjoyment. Finding the proper balance between these demands figures as one of the most difficult and important tasks World Heritage Site managers have to perform.

The World Heritage List resulted from a global treaty that seeks to identify, recognize and protect places that are of «outstanding universal value.» These fall into two main categories: human-made sites and natural sites. The former are often referred to as cultural sites, or historic sites, and they form the subject of this handbook. They include archaeological sites, ruins or intact structures still in use today or adapted for new purposes. In contrast to natural heritage sites, cultural sites contain the physical evidence of human creativity or serve as mute witnesses of major historical events. They record momentous achievements and put visitors in direct contact with an otherwise invisible past.

In only a few countries are sufficient funds allocated for educating and hiring staff for the professional care, maintenance and presentation of these great places. Yet glamorous pictures of World Heritage Sites are used in national tourism marketing campaigns, and visitors flock to them. Tourism earns hard currency and is the darling of national finance ministers. Conservation, however, is usually the last line-item to be included in national budgets and the first line-item to be cut.

This imbalance of national priorities requires immediate redress. In the year 1991, there were 450 million international tourist arrivals worldwide. In the year 2000, the figure is expected to rise to 650 million. The pressure on World Heritage Sites can only be expected to increase. When they were built, most of these sites were not meant for large numbers of people, and certainly they were not intended to accommodate thousands of tourists.

The management of World Heritage Sites is a crucial issue. This book is devoted to helping the managers of World Heritage Sites accomplish a dual purpose: to conserve the site given to their care and to provide meaningful and considerate access to as many visitors as the site can allow. In order to do this, site managers must work in partnership with professionals in the fields of planning, community development and tourism.

These professionals comprise a large network that penetrates into virtually every sector of society. It is important to be aware of the extent of this network, because it provides the connection between the World Heritage Sites and their visitors. In general, this network of professionals work in planning, research, development, marketing and education. We need their skills and their friendship.

There are investors, developers, architects, insurance companies and economic analysts who do much of their work behind the scenes. There are writers, consultants and academics whose careers revolve around the world of travel. There are suppliers who provide for every need—from uniforms and air conditioners to toothpicks and telephones. Trainers prepare chefs, airline pilots, managers and computer operators to do their jobs. Public officials serve in agencies that issue licenses, collect taxes and regulate standards. Others drive buses, do laundry, mix drinks and park cars. This universe of working people guides the engine of the tourism industry and makes it possible for people to visit World Heritage destinations, at all.

Conservation Precedes Tourism

This book makes a critical and fundamental assumption: that conservation precedes tourism. Conservation is a separate and prior activity that prepares the way for tourism development. If conservation planning is successful, then acceptable, dignified and profitable tourism will follow. By setting the right tone, conservation in partnership with tourism can contribute to the financial and social progress of a country. Once conservators have defined the limitations of visitor access to a site, tourism professionals can help to attract visitors, manage their stay and generate income for the continued conservation, protection, interpretation and maintenance of the site.

It is not easy to create such a balance, especially because conservation and tourism are in many respects opposite kinds of endeavors. Generally speaking, conservators preserve and tourists consume. There is a way to create a bridge between the two. This is by developing the concept and practice of comprehensive planning in relation to World Heritage Sites.

Cultural Tourism

The meaning of cultural tourism has changed over the last two centuries. From 1750-1850, cultural tourism referred to the practice of traveling around Europe to study the fine arts. The sons of English aristocrats would go on a Grand Tour in the company of tutors and return home «cultured.» In the subsequent century, cultural tourism was adopted by merchants who traveled in order to develop «class.» And finally, in the present era of jet-propelled mass travel, «cultural tourism» has become a popular phrase, one however that is often abused.

At its worst, cultural tourism has taken on a sanctimonious tone, standing for all that is good and constructive in tourism, involving music, the arts and ethnic exchange. It distinguishes itself from bad and destructive tourism that sells the allure of beaches and satisfies the cravings of the body. Yet this definition is too moralistic to be useful. The same tourist may one day visit a World Heritage Site and the next be found relaxing on a beach sipping an exotic mixed drink.

Rather, cultural tourism, also known as «niche» tourism, can today be defined more functionally—that is, by what it does and how. Firstly, cultural tourism is small, well-managed, educational and frequently up-market tourism. It offers a special sort of visit to a person with particular, often rarefied, interests. It is not wide-ranging, mass tourism but tourism dedicated to presenting or explaining some cultural idea. In the case of World Heritage Sites, the cultural ideas are expressed in the monuments and surrounding locations.

«Cultural tourists» or niche travelers themselves are a particular kind of people. They tend to be environmentally conscious, politically open-minded and appreciative of cultural differences. They probably travel frequently, are highly educated and bring a sharp intellectual and friendly energy to their encounters with foreigners. They do not buy souvenirs but prefer handicrafts, which they seek to learn about and see how they are made. They don't object to modest means of transportation if it is taking them to some remarkable place, and they don't mind a small, local hotel as long as it is clean. They also aren't reluctant to spend money as long as they get value in return. They are refined customers with a love of excellence, a taste for the authentic, and they do not tolerate mediocrity.

Some destinations still have a direct link with the history that lends them international fame—for example, the great churches in the Philippines continue to be in daily use. Other places have a more tenuous link—the Acropolis, for example, has little relationship to the contemporary religious or social structure of modern Greece. Still, Athens, along with Rome, Venice and Istanbul, has been a classic destination for niche travelers. Egypt has been attracting niche travelers to its archaeological wonders for centuries. The terra-cotta soldiers of Xian have been attracting this same breed of voyager to China. Everywhere the opportunities for developing cultural tourism are expanding, and World Heritage Sites offer particularly fertile ground.

Niche travelers come in small numbers, they spend a healthy sum of money, and they leave. They are, as a group, highly desirable visitors to the often fragile contexts of World Heritage Sites. To satisfy niche travelers, however, requires not only the patient work of the conservationist but also the experience of the tourism expert in providing the quality service niche travelers demand.

Limiting the Number of Visitors

World Heritage Site managers must anticipate a continued rapid rise in the world's population and the continued growth of the travel industry, predicted to be the world's leading business enterprise in the early years of the next century. They must recognize that the sites entrusted to their care will remain the same size. This means that the number of visitors has to be controlled. But how?

Hearst Castle, situated in a relatively remote part of California, provides one instructive example. From the very day of its opening, the site was managed with a reservation admission system. Tickets were issued for a particular time and a particular day, and they were expensive. Hearst Castle is a public state park, but its managers did not hesitate to limit the number of visitors and raising prices to cover expenses.

In too many countries, the priorities are reversed: tourism is being promoted before conservation. Many World Heritage Sites are in countries that simply do not have either the money or the expertise to meet international conservation standards. Even when there is a national awareness, financial support for even minimal conservation is 15 or 20 years away. There are too many other needs higher up on the national agenda. These countries need an interim plan that will initiate basic conservation steps. They need to match this plan with a tourism strategy that promotes their World Heritage Sites as magnets for only limited tourism.

Such a plan of action would help conserve the sites for future generations, while allowing access and appreciation for the present generation. Such a plan of action would help generate income for the national economy without endangering the national patrimony. In the future, World Heritage Sites may become the high-priced, hard-to-get-into attractions in the tourism world.

The World Heritage Convention requires that nations not only protect, conserve and rehabilitate World Heritage Sites; it also requires that these sites be given a role in the life of the community. The point is not to place these treasures under lock and key but to integrate them safely into the fabric of life. A dilemma exists that underscores the need for balance among the interests of venerable sites, local residents, and future groups of visitors. This handbook is meant to help World Heritage Site managers take a step in striking that balance.

Table of Contents

Editor' Notes:

* Current as of July 1996. For subsequent listings of sites on the World Heritage List, consult the World Heritage Center WebsiteÑ www.unesco.org/whc

** The ICOMOS Charter on Cultural Tourism is currently undergoing revision to be submitted for ratification at the ICOMOS Triennium in Mexico City in 1999.

PREPARING THE FOUNDATION

Chapter 1

The World Heritage Convention: An Overview

The World Heritage Convention, whose full title is "The Convention Concerning the Protection of the World Cultural and Natural Heritage," was adopted by UNESCO in 1972. Today (Julyy 1996) 146 countries are party to the convention, which enlists the nations of the world to recognize, inventory, and protect unique and irreplaceable properties of universal value. The Convention provides, for the first time, a permanent legal, administrative and financial framework for international cooperation in safeguarding humankind's cultural and natural heritage. It introduces the specific concept of a "world heritage" whose importance transcends all political and geographic boundaries. Because the Convention is the bedrock document of World Heritage Sites, this first chapter examines what it is and how it works. The full text of the Convention can be found in Appendix A.

It is important for the site manager to have a basic understanding of the legal relationship of national, state (provincial) and local governments to the World Heritage Convention because these relationships determine how governments can influence or control tourism at World Heritage Sites.

The World Heritage Lists

On signing the Convention, each country pledges to conserve those cultural and natural sites within its borders that are recognized by the Convention as being of exceptional and universal value. In return, the international community promises to help protect these treasures. To define these significant sites, the Convention has established the World Heritage List, which contains the cultural and natural properties that have met specific criteria defined by the World Heritage Committee. The first twelve sites were inscribed on the list in 1978. Currently there are 469 sites listed in 104 countries: 350 cultural sites, 102 natural sites and 17 mixed cultural and natural sites.

The World Heritage Committee also prepares and publishes a List of World Heritage in Danger, which includes World Heritage properties threatened with destruction, major alteration or abandonment. These threats may be caused by any one or combination of dangers including: accelerated deterioration, large-scale public or private projects, rapid urban and tourist development, changes in use or ownership, armed conflict, fires, earthquakes, landslides, volcanic eruptions, floods, tidal waves and changes in water levels. Each time the committee adds a new entry to the List of World Heritage in Danger, it is required to publicize the fact immediately.

The World Heritage Fund

Under the Convention, a Fund has been established for the Protection of World Cultural and Natural Heritage of Outstanding Universal Value. It is financed by contributions from member nations and from private organizations and individuals. The fund responds to requests by member countries for international cooperation in protecting their World Heritage Sites, as well as providing urgent conservation for properties on the danger list. Member nations can request international assistance from the fund for studies, expert consultations, technical advice, skilled labor, staff training and the supply of equipment for protection, conservation, rehabilitation and interpretation of World Heritage Properties. Member nations can also apply for long-term loans and, in special cases, for outright grants.

The level of the fund--$3 million (U.S.) for 1996-- may be far below what is required, but it has already financed important projects in Africa, Latin America, the Caribbean and Europe.

National and International Protection

Member countries recognize that they assume primary responsibility for safeguarding World Heritage properties in their countries. They agree to do all they can with their own resources and with international assistance. This includes agreement to:

- adopt a general policy giving cultural and natural heritage a role in the life of the community and integrate the protection of that heritage into comprehensive planning programs;
- set up mechanisms to protect, conserve and interpret that heritage;
- develop research studies and operating methods to counteract dangers to that heritage;
- take appropriate legal, scientific, technical, administrative and financial measures to preserve and present that heritage;
- foster national or regional training and research centers in the fields of conservation and interpretation.

It is the duty of the international community as a whole to cooperate in protecting world heritage; therefore member countries agree to help other countries when they ask for assistance in identifying, protecting and conserving their designated heritage sites. Also each country agrees not to take deliberate measures that might directly or indirectly damage another country's World Heritage properties.

The World Heritage Committee

The Convention is administered by a World Heritage Committee consisting of 21 nations elected from those nations that are party to the Convention. Elections are held every two years. The committee's main tasks are to:

- identify those nominated properties of outstanding universal value that are to be protected under the Convention and included on the World Heritage List;
- place threatened properties on the List of World Heritage in Danger;
- delete from the World Heritage List those properties that have lost their World Heritage status through damage or deterioration;
- administer the World Heritage Fund;
- inform the public about all of the above.

The executive body of the World Heritage Committee is the World Heritage Bureau. At its annual meeting, the Committee elects a chairman, five vice-chairmen and a rapporteur who hold office for one year.

The World Heritage Centre

UNESCO established the World Heritage Centre in 1992 to implement, rapidly and efficiently, activities related to the World Heritage Convention and more specifically to:

- encourage nonsubscribed states to join the Convention;
- encourage member countries to nominate sites to the World Heritage List;
- assist states in training competent staff for the management, protection and restoration of their country's cultural and natural heritage;

- help states prepare and implement conservation projects;
- mobilize extra-budgetary funds for this purpose;
- monitor the state of conservation of sites already inscribed on the list;
- respond promptly when armed conflict or natural and man-made disasters threaten World Heritage Sites;
- broadly promote UNESCO's efforts in the field of cultural and natural heritage to the general public and specialized audiences.

The World Heritage Logo

The logo (see frontispiece) symbolizes the interdependence of cultural and natural properties: the central square alludes to human creativity while the circle represents nature, the two being intimately linked. Round like the world, the emblem is at the same time a symbol of protection.

Government's Legislative Responsibilities

All levels of government may play a role in relation to tourism and cultural World Heritage Sites. The exact nature of this role may vary from country to country and from site to site depending on a range of factors including the respective government's philosophy and involvement in tourism and conservation.

However, so far as the protection and management of a cultural World Heritage Site is concerned, it is only the national government that is obliged to comply with the requirements of the World Heritage Convention. The Convention is only open to member countries of UNESCO and others invited by UNESCO to accede to it. Where a country has a federal or non-unitary form of government, the convention contains a specific provision to ensure that the national government is the "state party," the designation used in the convention. Article 34 requires the central or national government of a signatory country to have the same obligations as any other state party, even though it may not have the direct power under that country's constitution to deal with the World Heritage Site. They may delegate powers, depending upon the particular country's form of government, but they cannot delegate their ultimate responsibility to the international community.

The obligations the World Heritage Convention imposes on national governments relate to authenticity, management, education and protection. While the duties that must be performed to fulfill the obligations can be delegated by the national government to state and local authorities, the obligations remain, at an international level, those of the national government.

State and local governments may have responsibilities for World Heritage Sites or parts thereof. These responsibilities are only placed upon them because of the country's contribution or because of acts by the national government. If, however, the state or local government does not carry out its obligations, only the country's laws can be invoked against that level of government.

The Need for National Legislation

Proper management of World Heritage Sites may require all signatories to the Convention to consider enacting domestic legislation to regulate and control World Heritage Sites within their jurisdiction. This should be done under their respective constitutions or pursuant to their obligations under the Convention. This is an important issue, not just in relation to tourism but in relation to all activities within the country that may affect World Heritage Sites.

Despite the fact that more than 129 countries are signatories to the Convention, only Australia has enacted specific domestic legislation setting out the powers and responsibilities of the national government in relation to the Convention and World Heritage Sites within the country. The legislation is the 1983 World Heritage Properties Conservation Act, as amended by the Conservation Legislation Act of 1988.

There are provisions in the United States of America that clarify certain points: who shall coordinate U.S. participation in the Convention (the Secretary of the Interior); nomination procedures; and, perhaps most important of all, the stipulation that no property may be nominated unless it has previously been determined to possess national significance.

There is a brief mention of the Convention in the legislation of some other countries but by way of notification only, and there are no specific provisions setting out how the relevant national government shall comply with its obligations under the Convention.

Every country that is a signatory to the Convention should consider the enactment of legislation to: 1) bolster recognition of the Convention; 2) specifically and clearly empower a particular branch of government to enforce the protection of World Heritage Sites; and 3) improve the overall protection and conservation of such sites. This is particularly important in those countries (such as Australia), where by virtue of its constitution, the central government has no direct power to protect World Heritage Sites or otherwise comply with the terms of the Convention.

The World Heritage Convention and Tourism

Being listed as a World Heritage Site enhances a property's attractiveness to tourists. Thus it is in the interest of all to ensure that nothing is done to prejudice the listing. Everything possible should be done to improve the property in accordance with the standards adopted by the World Heritage Committee at the time of its inscription.

While tourism, as a substantial income earner, can frequently assist with the conservation of World Heritage Sites, it can also threaten their authenticity, preservation and proper management. Such threats must be taken seriously and resolved lest the country in question find itself in breach of its obligations under the Convention.

To guarantee successful tourism programs at World Heritage cultural sites, national governments should consider, at the outset of the nomination process, the requirements of the tourism infrastructure and whether or not these will result in compromising the listing of the sites. Similarly, subsequent introduction of tourism to sites already on the World Heritage List must only be undertaken with a clear understanding of the country's obligations under the World Heritage Convention for authenticity and the proper management of the site or sites in question.

Two major documents govern the operation of the World Heritage List. Site administrators of a World Heritage cultural site should have current copies of the World Heritage Convention adopted in 1972 (Appendix A) and the Operational Guidelines, last revised in February 1992 (Appendix B). Together they describe the process whereby a site gains election to the World Heritage List. This process is important to keep in mind when contemplating change as a result of tourism.

When a country submits a site for possible listing to the World Heritage Committee, the nomination must describe the monument's degree of authenticity and the level of management at the site. These constitute important criteria for consideration by the committee. Currently, no requirement exists for a listed site to obtain the approval of the World Heritage Committee before making changes that may affect the site's authenticity or its management. However, detrimental changes may result in a site's removal from the list.

Further, if such changes are perceived as breaches of the World Heritage Convention, they may result in international action against the national government. Depending upon the internal laws of the country, one or more of its citizens may take actions against the national government in order to require the offensive action to be rectified. Even though other authorities may govern a property's day-to-day management, there remains an overlying requirement to comply with the authenticity and management standards set by the World Heritage Committee at the time it inscribed the site on the World Heritage List.

Management Responsibilities

Under the Convention, a state party must protect cultural and natural properties of "outstanding universal value." The Operational Guidelines amplify this point:

> The convention provides for the protection of these cultural and natural properties deemed to be of outstanding universal value. It is not intended to provide for the protection of all properties of great interest, importance or value, but only for a select list of the most outstanding of these from an international viewpoint. The outstanding universal value of cultural and natural properties is defined by Articles 1 and 2 of the convention. These definitions are interpreted by the committee by using two sets of criteria: one set for cultural property and another set for natural property. [Paragraph 6 (i)]
>
> The fundamental principle stipulated in the convention is that properties nominated therefore should be carefully selected. The criteria and conditions of authenticity of integrity against which the committee will evaluate properties are set out in paragraphs 24 and 36. Within a given geo-cultural region, it may be desirable for States Parties to make comparative assessments for the harmonization of tentative lists and nominated cultural properties. Support for the organization of meetings for this purpose may be requested under the World Heritage Fund. [Paragraph 9]

Once outstanding properties have been identified and nominated, states parties must take appropriate protective measures as outlined in their nomination papers. Paragraph 22 of the guidelines clarifies this expectation:

> Where the intrinsic qualities of a nominated property are threatened by action of man and yet meet the criteria and the conditions of authenticity or integrity set out in paragraphs 24 and 36, an action plan outlining the corrective measures required should be submitted with the nomination file. Should the corrective measures submitted by the nominating State not be taken within the time proposed by the State, the property will be considered by the Committee for de-listing in accordance with the procedure adopted by the Committee. State Parties are encouraged to prepare plans for the management of each natural site nominated and for the safeguarding of each cultural property nominated. All information concerning these plans should be made available when technical cooperation is requested.

Under the Convention each state party undertakes to protect, conserve and present its cultural heritage and to participate in international agreements. Procedures and obligations to achieve these ends are enumerated in Articles 5 and 6 of the Convention (Appendix A).

Authenticity and Management

When a site is submitted for inclusion on the list, the committee looks carefully at its ability to maintain authenticity and ensure proper management, particularly in relation to tourism. The Operational Guidelines require that sites:

> ". . . meet the test of authenticity in design, materials, workmanship or setting (the

Committee stressed that reconstruction is only acceptable if it is carried out on the basis of complete and detailed documentation on the original and to no extent on conjecture)." [Paragraph 24(b) (i)]

"... and have adequate legal protection and management mechanisms to insure the conservation of the nominated cultural property. The existence of protective legislation at the national, provincial or municipal level is therefore essential and must be stated clearly on the nomination form. Assurance of the effective implementation of these laws are also expected. Furthermore, in order to preserve the integrity of cultural sites, particularly those open to large numbers of visitors, the State Party concerned should be able to provide evidence of suitable administrative arrangements to cover the management of the property, its conservation and its accessibility to the public." [Paragraph 24(b) (ii)]

Although not precise, these guidelines do establish a framework within which it is possible to judge whether proper standards are being maintained. In some cases, for example in relation to historic towns, the guidelines acknowledge the management problems and state that preference should be given to "small or medium-sized urban areas which are in a position to manage any potential growth." Further:

"In view of the effects which the entry of a town on the World Heritage List could have on its future, such entries should be exceptional. Inclusion in the List implies that legislative and administrative measures have already been taken to insure the protection of the group of buildings and its environment." [Paragraph 33]

It may be necessary to control additional areas to ensure that the property receives adequate protection, as the guidelines recommend:

"Whenever necessary for the proper conservation of a cultural or natural property nominated, an adequate 'buffer zone' around a property should be provided and should be afforded the necessary protection. A buffer zone can be defined as an area surrounding the property which has restrictions placed on its use to give an added layer of protection; the area constituting the buffer zone should be determined in each case through technical studies. Details on the size, characteristics and authorized uses of a buffer zone, as well as a map indicating its precise boundaries, should be provided in the nomination file relating to the property in question." [Paragraph 17]

The national government may need to delegate the responsibility to properly manage a buffer zone to a state or local authority. In doing so, of course, the national government should ensure that the management plan for the buffer zone is compatible with that of the World Heritage Site.

Juridical Provisions

Among the nomination documents a country submits to the World Heritage Committee are those of a juridical nature. This information details the laws that protect the nominated property and shows how they are implemented. The guidelines stipulate:

"Under the 'Juridical data' section of the nomination form States Parties should provide, in addition to the legal texts protecting the property being nominated, an explanation of the way in which these laws actually operate. Such an analysis is preferable to a mere enumeration or compilation of the legal text themselves." [Paragraph 11]

Guideline 54(b), in reference to a paragraph entitled Responsible Administration, asks for the following juridical information:

Owner
Legal Status

- category of ownership (public or private)
- details of legal and administrative provisions for the protection of the property. The nature of the legal text as well as their conditions of implementation should be clearly specified.
- state of occupancy and accessibility to the general public.

Responsible administration

- details should be given of the mechanism or body already set up or intended to be established in order to insure the proper management of the property.

Paragraph 54 (f) also requires the following information:

Legal information

- laws or decrees that govern the protection of monuments and sites (date and text)
- decrees or orders that protect the nominated property (date and text)
- master plan for historic preservation, land-use plan, urban development plan, regional development plan or other infrastructure projects
- town planning regulations and orders issued in application of these plans.

Further, indications should be given as to whether various juridical provisions prevent:

- uncontrolled exploitation of the ground below the property
- the demolition and reconstruction of buildings situated within the protected zones
- the raising of the height of buildings
- the transformation of the urban fabric.

What are the penalties foreseen in case of a contravention of these juridical provisions? What, if any, juridical or other measures exist that encourage the revitalization of the property concerned in full respect of its historic authenticity and its social diversity?

There is also a responsibility to comply with the laws or regulations within the particular country to protect the World Heritage Site(s). These laws may have been passed pursuant to power that the national government acquired as a result of becoming a signatory to the World Heritage Convention or just because control of the site forms part of the country's national laws.

There are countries such as Australia, Canada and the United States with federal systems of government where, by virtue of its laws or written constitution, the national government does not have jurisdiction over measures required under the Convention. Regardless of how the internal government of the particular country is organized, the national government must assume those powers to ensure a site's protection and meet the convention's requirements.

What this means in simple terms is that the country's national government has a two-fold responsibility: 1) to comply with the World Heritage Convention (this obligation cannot be delegated to another level of government); and 2) to ensure that those actions necessary to comply with the

Convention are taken. This responsibility can be delegated, although the national government will remain ultimately responsible to the Convention.

Only those nominations that meet these requirement can be considered for listing by the World Heritage Committee. Failure to comply with these two responsibilities may result in the loss of outstanding universal value and, in theory, may lead the World Heritage Committee to remove a property from the list.

Chapter 2

Establishing a Management Philosophy

The first step in the care of World Heritage Sites is the development and implementation of a management philosophy. The effort to formulate the principles upon which the site will be administered lays the foundation for all that happens subsequently. In general, two areas of concern must be addressed--conservation and accessibility. What are the values of the site that require protection, and how will protection be guaranteed? And, how can the site be made safely accessible to an appropriate number of visitors and its significance clearly communicated?

Creating a management philosophy requires study, exchange and reflection. It is a planning process in which openness to ideas and possibilities is the key. This chapter reviews the essential elements of establishing a tourism-related management philosophy.

Type of Site and Its Use

The core of any management plan is to decide what types of activities are going to be allowed at the site. The administrative team must first consider the nature of the site and understand its physical characteristics and cultural significance. The team must be sensitive to the way the site has been shaped and assembled to achieve specific forms and spatial relationships. It must also understand that its historic fabric needs to be preserved unaltered in perpetuity. With this understanding, planning for the needs of visitors can follow smoothly.

If it is decided to provide visitor accommodations on the site, it is imperative that all planning, financial decisions and agreements support the integrity of the site. Final authority with regard to the location and operation of such facilities must be retained by the site administration.

The site administration should participate in all public planning and land-use processes that affect the site and its surrounding areas. It is important to be mindful of all types of land use including those that relate to major traffic corridors leading to the site and especially areas that are visible from the site. Uncontrolled, insensitive, speculative and commercial development around a site can easily lead to negative consequences. Private developers of hotels will usually seek close proximity to a site and, if possible, maximal views of the site from their location.

Conservation Policy

When developing a conservation policy, it helps to consult the major international documents prepared over the last three decades to preserve the world's heritage. The ICOMOS Venice Charter provides an excellent set of guidelines for evaluation, planning and decision making in conservation work. Adopted in 1964 at the Second International Congress of Architects and Technicians of Historic Monuments, the charter has been adapted by some countries such as Australia in their "Guidelines to the Burra Charter: Conservation Policy" and in the U.S. as "The Secretary of the Interior's Standards for Historic Preservation Projects."

Yet because the need was felt for guidelines that applied more specifically to other than monumental sites, international specialists worked for twelve years to develop the "ICOMOS Charter on the Conservation of Historic Towns and Urban Areas," which was adopted at the 1987 ICOMOS General Assembly in Washington D.C.

A sound conservation policy requires that all conservation activities be carefully balanced. In particular, the following factors must be addressed: 1) protection of the resources from human-caused erosion, destruction, damage and alteration by controlling and limiting visitor access to the site; 2) conservation of the historic fabric through appropriate housekeeping and maintenance; and 3) conservation of the site's historic character by excluding or limiting inappropriate activities within it.

One of the principal threats facing sites is the failure to plan for mass tourism, which can, through erosion, vandalism or inadvertent effects, create conditions that accelerate deterioration or even destroy a site. Damage tends to be greater in enclosed interior spaces, but, in reality, no area of a site is invulnerable. The sources of damage, though varied, are surprisingly uncomplicated: the erosive effect of shoes on historic floors, pavements and steps; damage to surfaces from grease deposited by hands repeatedly touching or by heads repeatedly leaning against the fabric or paper of a wall.

Archaeological sites particularly fall prey to souvenir collectors who remove pieces of the historic fabric as mementos. Without conservation planning, archaeological sites can suffer great damage from repeated trampling by visitors. Delicate areas, or areas yet to be fully excavated, should have tour patterns clearly demarcated and roped off.

Materials and finishes of enclosed interior spaces are particularly vulnerable to drastic humidity and temperature fluctuations caused by the sudden entrance and exit of masses of people who exude large amounts of heat and water vapor. All hygroscopic materials--wood, textiles, some stones, plaster, etc.--are vulnerable to constant shifts in air quality. Damage from this source has caused the closing to the public of important prehistoric cave sites such as Lascaux, as well as decorated underground burial vaults. Sometimes, it is possible to open windows to promote a more stable environment through natural ventilation, but this often adds problems such as an increase in dust deposits, ultraviolet-ray damage and potential infestation.

Furniture and other large objects that make up the contents of a World Heritage cultural site need protection from visitors. Like architectural materials, moveable objects can deteriorate from continuous fluctuations of environmental conditions. Unless extremely sturdy, historic furniture must not be placed in areas where it will be subjected to use by large numbers of people. Chairs and other seats should be roped and all other furniture removed from the reach of the hands of visitors. Discreet signs requesting "Do not touch exhibits" should be displayed.

As with all cultural property, small objects and artifacts are subject to environmental deterioration, especially those made of organic materials and certain metals. Small objects can fall prey to petty theft and must be protected. When installing security systems, management should avoid those that damage the object through the adherence or insertion of detection strips or other monitoring elements.

Mechanical ventilation systems, especially those using forced air, are designed to maintain an ideal interior climate. Forced air heating/air conditioning ventilation systems (HVAC) for historic buildings and museums often feature sophisticated devices that control humidity and temperature fluctuations in response to varying conditions inside and outside the building. When the maximum number of people visiting a building is exceeded, the HVAC system may no longer operate properly. If the situation is repeated over long periods of time, both the system and the historic fabric may begin to deteriorate rapidly. For this reason, it is important that heritage site administrators and the site's engineering staff consult designers and manufacturers of the ventilation system so that all understand the necessary limits of a building's visitation.

Cultural heritage sites are inextricably linked to their surrounding traditional environment. In fact, this ambiance often forms an integral part of the cultural site and may consist of historic gardens and landscapes. Sites with unusually large visitation or with fragile botanical collections should declare all planted areas off-limits and have them be only visually accessible. Introduction of fences and other physical barriers, even if largely transparent, must be approached with great caution, especially if no historical precedent exists for their use. Too many limitations placed on physical access, aggressively presented, can disfigure the character of the site and create a false impression unrelated to its true significance. If economically feasible, discreet signs and the presence of guards are always preferable to highly visible extraneous devices to control the unwanted wanderings of visitors.

Relationships with Living Communities

When sites are also living communities, those areas dedicated to visitors must be carefully planned. Permanent residents must be given respect. Visitors must not be allowed to interfere with the daily lives of residents nor their interactions with the site. This is usually accomplished by designating sections of the site off-limits to visitors, either during certain hours or at all times. This will help to avoid mutual animosities, unflattering comparisons and deformation of traditional behavior, crafts and culture. In historic villages, especially, the resident community often has limited economic resources when contrasted to the tourists. Planners must anticipate a potential clash of values and behavior between residents and tourists.

Types of Visitors

World Heritage cultural sites by definition are of significance to all humanity. Nevertheless, some sites attract specific groups of people for religious, patriotic, professional or other reasons. Site management should provide access and design tours, exhibits, interpretative programs and printed information that satisfies the interests of each type of visitor. In order to do so, the first step is to establish a visitor profile. Who is the typical visitor? Basic socio-economic data--age, nationality, income, marital status, profession, etc.--can provide a clear picture of the typical visitor. (See Chapter 7 of this handbook, "Recording and Analyzing Visitor Data.")

At times it is difficult to transmit the significance of a site to some sectors of the public. For archaeological and battlefield sites in particular, a paucity of visual materials and artifacts often precludes an easy grasp of their significance by many nonspecialist visitors. This situation requires a more intense interaction between visitors and guides, as well as more extensive exhibits and explanations to make the site intelligible.

The provenance of visitors is also important, especially if large groups are foreigners. They will require site interpretation in different languages. If visitors are largely local, site-related cultural-community programs can provide an alternative to elaborate interpretative programs. For local youth, it is recommended that the site management team work closely with educators to institute site-awareness programs. This way the children may be encouraged to grow up to be stewards of the site.

It is also useful to know the economic status of visitors in order to assess the feasibility of instituting fees for admission, interpretative programs, special events and other services. Most sites also have small souvenir and information shops, whose merchandise must be geared to the consumption patterns of typical visitors.

Carrying Capacity and Access

Determining the carrying capacity and level of access for a site can be a complicated and sensitive undertaking. The first step is to analyze the site to determine the optimum number of visitors who can be present at any one time. This includes a plan to schedule group visits in an orderly fashion. Secondly, the management team must determine site access--which areas are of interest to the visitor profile groups. These areas must then be compared to those that the management team considers to be of primary significance. Then the team must decide what areas are essential for visitors to see.

The team must then plan for different levels of visitor interest. Some tourists are satisfied with a cursory visit. Others may desire a detailed interpretation and a comprehensive tour. Some sites attract a large number of scholars. For each case, the management team must determine the optimal number of visitors allowed in each area at any one time.

The amount of accessible floor area clearly provides the most direct limit upon the number of people who can visit a building site at any one time. No specific formula exists, however, to determine the ideal ratio between the number of visitors and the building's floor space. Spatial considerations, conservation concerns, safety precautions, visibility and accommodation of children are but a few of the factors that influence the allowable number of people occupying the site.

Visits to interior spaces present more difficulties than do exterior areas. Consideration must be given to noise level, climate control and security when large numbers of people occupy and move through interior spaces. If the areas, both indoor and outdoor, are ample, then the need for a rigid tour pattern is not so urgent. Another concern is the flow of visitors through a site: should it be a constant stream or organized in groups?

If the site can accommodate more than the current visitor load, management should consider creating a plan to increase their number and determine how the site will deal with increased visitation. Depending on their nature, some sites lend themselves to unrestricted access with little structure and no time limits. Other sites require more stringent rules that may consist of specific tour routes, group visits of limited numbers, or even mandatory guided supervision.

All cultural heritage sites must provide some kind of tour, either with a guide or self-directed by means of signage, audio cassettes or printed materials. Depending on the site, tours can be optional or obligatory, free or available for a fee. Care should be given in designing supervised tours to make sure all visitors can hear the guide and have an opportunity to ask questions. If visitors tend to arrive in large groups at a particular time of the day, design guided tours of specific duration. A 30-45 minute wait is about the maximum visitors will tolerate. If longer waits are necessary, issue tickets for a specific hour, so that visitors can then explore the site on their own until the appointed time.

Tour operators may need to make special arrangements with site management to avoid a visitor glut. Also, management should decide whether and how to grant access to restricted areas to outside guides.

Security and Insurance Considerations

The prevention of possible injury to visitors must rank high in any site management plan. Management should periodically inspect all areas open to the public to ensure that safe conditions prevail. Hazardous and restricted areas must be clearly marked through internationally recognized signage. Areas that present danger or house valuable collections should have intrusion alarm systems. When designing tour routes, make sure to study the safety of the path: it must have adequate width and overhead clearance, railings at significant level changes, clearly marked steps, etc. In addition, consider the effect visitors will have along the route. Will large numbers of visitors create hazards that do not currently exist, such as structural overload and insufficient fresh air?

Smoking inside historic structures must be strictly forbidden. Aside from being a fire hazard, the tar in tobacco smoke can damage historic surfaces, finishes and collections. In open-air archaeological sites and in historic gardens and landscapes, smoking should be discouraged to avoid littering. If smoking is allowed, provide unobtrusive, yet abundant ashtrays. Hand-held automatic fire extinguishers should be discreetly located throughout historic structures and staff should be instructed in their use.

In many countries, when visitors enter a site, its administration becomes legally responsible for their welfare and liable for any injury that befalls the visitor. In these cases, usually management has secured insurance policies to cover themselves in the event of accidents and resulting law suits. These policies often delineate numerous conditions the site must meet and enforce for the policy to be in effect. It is imperative for site managers to study existing policies and discuss with insurance carriers the extent and type of protection a policy offers, as well as the conditions under which a policy can become invalidated.

Visitor Services

A cultural heritage site must be able to accommodate not only visitors but also the many maintenance workers who come to the site to service its infrastructure. The construction and location of all visitor-service equipment must combine visitor convenience with minimal visual impact and not take away from or disturb the historic character and fabric of the site.

Provision for visitor services often depends on the proximity of a site to companies or agencies that deliver them. Remote sites may need to make arrangements for visitors to purchase meals and even provide overnight accommodations. Offering such services involves the added complications of food and equipment delivery, laundry service, etc. Similarly, remote site administrators must make sure that sufficient services exist to maintain safety and cleanliness, such as first-aid medical treatment, fire-fighting and police service, trash removal, clean running water, sewers, electricity and telecommunications.

Among the most visually disruptive services a cultural site must provide is vehicular parking. Another is the provision of toilets. Both services are crucial to visitor comfort. The first step in managing both parking services and toilets is determining the need, then deciding on discreet placement.

Tour buses, because of their size, need special shielding made up of vegetation or landscaped walls and fences. If the site cannot provide adequate parking, consider using remote locations with courtesy shuttle transportation.

Large sites should provide toilet facilities in more than one location, and always near restaurants or snack areas. Toilet facilities should have running water and be connected to an appropriate sewer system. Under extraordinary circumstances, self-contained chemical toilet booths, such as those found at construction sites, are preferable to none at all. Unless designed as individual units, group toilets with banks of fixtures are to be segregated by gender. Additional facilities should be provided for families with small children and for visitors with disabilities. There should be individual units with WC and lavatory, plus sufficient space for a wheelchair to maneuver plus an assistant or traveling companion, potentially of the opposite sex. For family-oriented sites, an area should be designed for a parent of either sex to change a baby's diapers. It is usual to have such a changing station in both the men's and women's restrooms.

Special Considerations: Historic Towns and Urban Areas

The management of urban historic sites can be extremely complex. They are living organisms, often densely populated, with deteriorating infrastructures and enormous developmental pressures. Management of these sites is often divided up among various local and national government agencies that control a variety of urban functions: public services, zoning, public improvements, utilities, demolition and construction permits, land use, etc. The only adequate methodology for managing tourism and preservation in historic towns and urban areas is through a planning process than invites the cooperation and coordination of all involved agencies.

Often tourism promotion is shared by many groups for different reasons. The site management team must clearly espouse and defend the cultural values of the site to avoid demeaning commercialization, damage to the historic fabric and other inappropriate developments. The site management team must meet periodically with representatives from other organizations to discuss the changing needs of visitors and local inhabitants. The team also must set clear limitations on the activities that each agency can undertake inside the town or urban area.

The complexities of managing and preserving historic towns and urban areas are too extensive to be dealt with here comprehensively. There are a few considerations, however, that demand mention. One of the most important has to do with traffic and parking. Vehicular congestion has a large impact on both the residents' quality of life and the tourist's visit. It is probably best for visiting tourists to leave their vehicles outside the historic zone at a surface-level or multistory garage facility outside the historic zone. The site management team must negotiate with transit authorities to identify special areas for visitor parking and to establish routes and schedules of tour buses. Clearly defined pedestrian routes and possible shuttle service should be provided to move the visitor from the parking locations to within the zone and back again. If visitor parking is provided within the historic zone, it should be limited and available at a considerable fee. In historic zones with new construction or reconstruction, provision should be made, if structurally possible, for underground parking garages. Generally, such parking facilities should be available on a priority basis for residents and businesses within the historic zone.

In those situations where a reasonable amount of street parking is available, a system should be adopted that allows property owners and renters to park on a priority basis and to be identifiable to the authorities through special stickers. Tourist parking should be limited to specific times and posted.

It may be desirable to temporarily close to auto, truck and bus traffic those streets that are most frequented by visitors. Any such temporary traffic ban must allow for quick access of emergency vehicles. Closure can be made with attractively designed moveable gates or metal stanchions.

Generally, large tour and airport buses should be discouraged from traveling through urban historic zones to pick-up or discharge passengers because of their potential negative impact on the physical fabric of the area (especially when turning tight corners). They also contribute to visual and environmental problems and require large amounts of space. Generally, it is wise to restrict them to defined areas on the periphery of the historic zone. Smaller shuttle vehicles should be used to move hotel guests and tour participants to centralized collection points on the periphery of the zone. If tour buses are to be allowed within the historic zone, they should be restricted in number and confined to specific streets and travel routes. If they are to park temporarily within such a zone, they need to be kept well away from historic monuments because of the pollution created by their exhaust emissions.

Another factor that demands consideration is commercialization within a historic zone. It is likely that a historic urban zone with a World Heritage designation will become a magnet for international visitors and local area residents. The concentration of large numbers of people will in turn attract business operators who seek to reach this lucrative market with their services and wares. Musicians, painters, mimes and puppeteers will be among those wishing to entertain visitors and solicit donations. To control their numbers and performance venues, they should be licensed and assigned to specific areas where they can perform. Musicians who perform for extended periods and at a loud volume can quickly generate strong opposition from local residents, businesses and visitors. Some historic urban zones have legally instituted maximum decibel levels for performers.

Historic zones can come under intense pressure to convert commercial businesses into restaurants and bars that feature entertainment. In climates where such facilities are often open to the outdoors, the existence of musical entertainment can easily create conflicts with neighboring residential and commercial districts. Local regulations may be needed to enforce the sound levels of outdoor entertainment. There must be a plan; if there is a problem, the plan has failed and must be revised.

Private organizations and public agencies wishing to sponsor festivals, fairs and special exhibits may want to use large public outdoor spaces in historic areas as venues for their events. If permitted, a set of written operating policies and guidelines should be prepared and available to the sponsors. Guidelines should address topics such as hours of access and departure, maximum public attendance, crowd-control procedures, security and sanitation, insurance requirements, restrictions on types and locations of temporary structures such as tents and booths, and use of temporary advertising signs associated with the event.

Chapter 3

The Site Managment Planning Process

To conserve the values for which a cultural site is placed on the World Heritage List, the World Heritage Convention requires that a nominating nation submit a management plan for its nominees. Such plans should consider the proper level of visitor access and tourism at the site. Conservation plans are best prepared by impartial experts with a broad knowledge of management issues related to protecting the site's value. As part of this effort, it is important that governments include World Heritage Sites within their national land-use planning process and recognize their global importance. At the local level, the site manager must monitor development decisions and their implementation at the site and its surrounding area.

Obligations under the Convention

The operational guidelines of the World Heritage Convention state that a national government tas on an obligation to maintain a site according to a general management plan, or, in the absence of a plan, to support the process of preparing and submitting one acceptable to the World Heritage Committee.

This plan does not have to fit within, or even have any regard for, the national or state or local planning system. It is for this reason that the Convention is such a powerful conservation instrument. While local authorities should be involved in the plan's formulation, they can only prepare plans to the extent that they have been delegated to do so by the national government making the nomination. World Heritage Sites are the one type of site where control is intentionally moved to the national level so that local authorities cannot operate independently. This philosophy runs counter to most other cases.

The World Heritage Convention stipulates the following in regard to planning:

- The national government must prepare an acceptable plan for the World Heritage Cultural Site to protect the values for which it is nominated.
- Nominations will not be accepted by the World Heritage Committee unless it includes an acceptable plan, submitted by the national government.
- Where such a plan does not exist for earlier entries on the World Heritage List, the national government in question should support the process to prepare and submit such plans.
- If a plan does not exist, the site administrator should actively encourage the national government to commit resources to prepare one.

The Planning Process

The planning process has three steps: 1) taking an inventory of existing resources; 2) categorizing and evaluating those resources; and, 3) based on that evaluated inventory, determining priorities for legislation, finances, personnel, equipment, conservation, interpretation and marketing.

Help in planning for a World Heritage Site is available from many sectors. Various appropriate government agency planning staffs can participate in the preparation of a site management and development plan. Furthermore, within most countries, land-use planning has become one of the mandated requirements of the World Bank and the International Monetary Fund. As a result, community planning and development skills have developed in the offices of health, environmental and economic agencies.

There also may be useful tourism management skills that are not being drawn into problem-solving at World Heritage Sites. For instance, the planning, design and management of large resorts draw on the same skills needed for site planning and management. Obviously there are different goals for a World Heritage Site and a resort. Yet, the issues of efficiency, security and visitor satisfaction are the same for both. Other tourism-related specialists can help, too. National airline and hotel executives know the economic value of World Heritage Sites and have in-house professionals whose skills, leadership and financial and political influence can assist the management and planning process.

Basic Planning Requirements

Cultural sites need a comprehensive regulatory plan, which includes:

- **Boundary Survey and Description:**
  The description of the listed site's boundaries should be clear. Wherever possible an appropriate buffer zone should also be designated to help protect the site. For planning purposes, the buffer should be treated as if it were part of the listed property even though the intensity of application of controls may be less.

- **Land Use Plan:**
  A comprehensive land-use plan for the site should include any nearby settlements and the vehicular corridor linking the site to the nearest urban center. For example, the quality of the road trip from Yogyakarta to Borobodur in Indonesia or from Chichen Itza to Merida and Cancun in Mexico is crucial to the visitors' overall experience.

  At urban sites, boundary lines and buffer zones should be drawn to protect historic streetscapes. In a rural setting, strong visual elements such as hills, tree lines, old roads and walls should be included within the boundaries. Both sides of any road, river or stream used as a borderline should be included if they are within the same country.

- **Conservation/Site Plan:**
  At World Heritage Sites the conservation plan is crucial. While the official submission of a site management plan is the responsibility of the national government, the site's administrator should actively participate in its preparation. The conservation plan delineates all pertinent conservation issues, analyzes them and determines scientifically the limitations of the site. The plan also outlines the administrator's concept of tourism at the site. Based on this plan, tourism professionals can assist and coordinate other planning elements.

- **A Utilities and Services Plan:**
  Both conservation and tourism management depend on utilities and services such electricity, sewers, water, telephones and fire and police protection. Although important, they should never jeopardize a site's integrity. Establish requirements and limits to guarantee that the delivery of current and projected utilities does not damage the site.

- **A Community Development Plan:**
  The quality of life for the residents within or adjacent to a site has a great impact on the quality of the visitors' experience. Whether an urban neighborhood or a rural village, what is good for visitors must also be good for residents.

  Make use of the government's community-development staffs of skilled professionals who are consulted when planning the delivery of medical services, sanitation, housing and schools. They are involved as well in agricultural support, development of cottage industries and family planning.

  Many countries have instituted job-training programs to prepare local residents to work in the tourism sector. Site managers and tourism planners, therefore, can be important partners in community development.

- **A Tourism Plan:**
  Tourism officials should be consulted when preparing the conservation plan, but the tourism plan itself should be one of the last considerations of the planning process. Tourism planners must recognize the goals, physical limits and visitor opportunities inherent in all other aspects of the plan. It must address: 1) transportation to and from, as well as within the site; 2) the full range of guest services--accommodations, food, toilet facilities, etc.; and 3) site tours, training and licensing guides, provision of travel information and interpretation; 4) museum installations, visitor paths, information signs, admission kiosks and sales outlets for film, postcards, stamps and souvenirs.

- **Coordinating Conservation and Tourism Plans:**
  All too often land-use plans have allowed the construction of unsightly multistory buildings, badly situated parking lots, or the forced relocation of long-time residents. Coordinating conservation and tourism planning can help eliminate the chances of similar tragedies. When a country nominates a site to the World Heritage List, it must also mobilize the nation's full resources to conserve, protect and present it. If site administrators, conservators, community leaders and tourism officials see themselves as part of a larger, comprehensive planning process, risks and waste can be avoided.

Building a Structure

Chapter 4

Staffing and Budgeting

Any site, large or small, requires a staff who devote all or part of their salaried time to the site's visitors. They may be the men and women who order supplies, answer the phones and respond to mail, sell tickets, clean the grounds and pay the bills. A well-organized staff greatly enhances the quality of a visit to a World Heritage Site. This chapter considers four different categories of staffing needs--administration, visitor services, maintenance and security. It also examines budgetary matters because accurate records of income and expenses form an important management tool.

Staffing

The individuals filling administrative positions are responsible for the overall quality and management of the site. The following lists a representative sample of administrative positions likely to be found at a site:

The Director: Develops and recommends all visitor-related policies and procedures to the governing authority. He or she also is responsible for the overall planning, management, budgeting and evaluation of all visitor-related programs and activities. The director also prepares job descriptions, conducts interviews, hires and evaluates staff working in visitor-related areas.

- **The Curator:**
  Ensures the accuracy of all interpretive materials made available to visitors. He or she works closely with the Conservator who is charged with the responsibility to ensure that all the site's valuable resources and artifacts are adequately protected.
- **The Concession Manager:**
  Sees that concession service providers (of food, transport, security, crafts and publications) adhere to the site's governing policies. The concession manager prepares contracts, bids and tenders for all visitor services, evaluating them and making recommendations to the director. He or she also monitors and ensures that service providers meet performance and quality standards.
- **The Office Manager:**
  Responsible for personnel, financial matters, payroll, supply and communication functions related to visitor services.

A typical visitor services staff consists of the following:

- **Information Clerk:**
  The first person a visitor is likely to encounter is the information clerk, who is responsible for providing basic printed and verbal information about the site. Multilingual skills may be required.
- **Admission Sales Clerk:**
  Responsible for the maintenance and operation of ticket sales.
- **Guides:**
  Provides personal verbal interpretation of the site to all visitors. Multilingual skills may be required.
- **Shop Manager:**
  Responsible for the overall management of visitor-related shops--inventory, stocking, display, sales, record-keeping and reporting.

- **Sales Clerk:**
  Reports to the shop manager and provides sale services to visitors.
- **Stock Clerk:**
  Maintains the shop inventory and restocks the sales areas.

To provide adequate Security, the site must have a well-trained staff of guards.

- **Guard:**
  Provides security day and night. They must often be trained to operate site-protection systems and should possess adequate skills to deal with the visiting public in a polite yet purposeful manner. Background checks should be made with local police departments on all prospective guards. In some cases, guards must know how to use firearms and/or handle guard dogs. For large sites with many guards, it may be useful to adopt a military-like organizational structure with a rank of captain, sergeants, lieutenants, etc.

For sites with large numbers of visitors, certain members of the Maintenance staff may be assigned to work only in visitor-related services.

- **Foreman:**
  Responsible for planning, organizing, supervising and evaluating the work of subordinate staff.
- **Engineer:**
  Responsible for the maintenance and operation of all mechanical systems related to visitor services--electrical, HVAC, plumbing, etc.
- **Laborer/Cleaner:**
  Responsible for daily servicing of all visitor areas--trash collection, storage and removal, cleaning and restocking of public facilities.
- **Gardener:**
  Looks after public garden areas. Increasingly, gardens or landscapes in and around World Heritage Sites attempt to duplicate historic designs, or at least introduce appropriate plants and trees.

Budgeting

All sites open to the public will have both income and expenditures that must be tracked accurately. Income is earned from many sources and funds are spent in many different ways. It is important, therefore, for planning purposes to record the different kinds of income and expenditure on separate lines. Then a manager can see at a glance how much income was earned from ticket sales, or how much was spent on entertainment. A manager can also use the budget to make decisions--how best to increase income, for example, or cut expenditures. The following serve as a basic checklist of possible budget line items.

The Income Budget

Money coming into a site is reflected in the income budget, which should be reviewed regularly during the fiscal year in order to monitor actual performance against the planned budget. In preparing the annual budget, it is useful to include the projected and actual budget performances of five previous years. This information can help identify income trends. There also should be a clear understanding what revenues can be kept at the site and how much has to be forwarded to a central office or a controlling national government agency.

- **Appropriations:**
  The funds allocated from public funds by local, state and/or national government authorities.
- **Grants-in-Aid:**
  The funds received as a grant from a public governmental body or international institution.

Admissions: The receipts from the site's paying visitors. For record-keeping, budgeting and long-range planning purposes, it is useful to account for admissions by category--adult, child, student, senior citizen, group, complimentary, etc.

- **Donations:**
  The funds received from solicited and unsolicited donations from private and public organizations. Individual projects or activities may be the target of special fund-raising appeals. Donors may restrict the use of donated funds for specific purposes. This should be clearly noted. Income from visitor donation boxes should also be included as a budget line-item.
- **Memberships:**
  The funds received from individuals and/or organizations paying an annual fee, which entitles the member to free admission and other benefits such as invitations to special events and publications.
- **Interest:**
  The funds earned by the site on its financial deposits and investments. It is wise to keep cash related to visitor income in interest-bearing checking and/or savings accounts. For security reasons, if daily receipts at a site are substantial, deposits should be made every day. It is possible to earn different types of interest, depending on whether the deposit is short, medium or long term. Managers should plan cash deposits and project future needs to maximize interest earned.
- **Property Rentals:**
  The funds earned from renting a site's buildings, areas or grounds for purposes that are compatible with a set policy. At sites with many buildings, there may be rental income from housing, food services, shops, and guest houses. Some sites may earn income from leasing agricultural land, grazing fees or forest usage.
- **Rental Fees for Special Property Uses:**
  The funds received from the use of any part of the site by an outside organization for receptions, dinners, performances, festivals, fairs, movie production, etc.
- **Contractual Services:**
  The funds received in exchange for the provision of a specified service--replication of period furniture, printing and reprinting a publication, technical services etc.
- **Licensing Fees and Royalties:**
  The funds, usually derived over a long period of time, from the payment of an up-front fee and a continuing royalty on all sales of significant site items that have been authentically replicated such as period furniture, historical fabric, architectural ornaments, garden sculpture, etc.
- **Sales of Items and Services:**
  The funds received from the sale of everything made available to the visitor within the site: postcards, publications, souvenirs, film, food, beverages and accommodations.
- **Sales and/or Service Taxes:**
  The funds received from the collection of all sales taxes applied to items and/or services provided at the site. Many sites will be legally required to collect these taxes and forward them to a government authority. Taxes should be separately accounted for-- sales, meals, room occupancy, beverage, etc.

The Expense Budget

Cash expended to operate a site, pay the employees, provide for security, etc., is reflected in the expense budget. The expense budget should be monitored monthly to measure actual expenditures against projected budgets. Line-items commonly include:

- **Staff Salaries:**
  The funds necessary to pay the regular, part-time and overtime salaries of the site's staff.

- **Staff Benefits:**
  The funds necessary to pay for the approved benefits available to salaried employees. These may include travel benefits, health and dental insurance premiums, retirement plan contributions, worker's compensation, annual vacation, sick and family leave.
- **Rent and Utilities:**
  The funds necessary to pay for rented space and utilities, which may include water, electricity, telephone and heat.
- **Insurance:**
  The funds used to purchase insurance premiums to protect the site administration and officials in cases of visitor accidents, legal actions, theft and property damage.
- **Equipment:**
  The funds used to purchase, service and run equipment required to accommodate visitors.
- **Capital Projects:**
  The funds used to construct, maintain, preserve, or restore visitor-related facilities.
- **Maintenance Service Contract Fees:**
  The funds used to retain contractors to regularly inspect and service any equipment such as elevators, computers, security alarm systems, etc.
- **Travel:**
  The funds used to pay for approved staff travel related to visitor services, for example, participation in training programs, attendance at conferences, etc.
- **Advertising:**
  The funds used to design and pay for public advertisements in the print and electronic media.
- **Printing Services:**
  The funds used to print materials given or sold to visitors.
- **Consultant Contracts and Fees:**
  The funds used to pay for professional consultant services related to any aspect of visitor services.
- **Security Equipment:**
  The funds used to acquire and operate site security systems, equipment and services.
- **Sales Stock Purchases:**
  The funds used to purchase items sold to visitors at site outlets.
- **Entertainment and Hospitality:**
  The funds used to receive and entertain important visitors to the site and for staff parties, receptions for volunteers, community leaders and media representatives.

Chapter 5

Policies on Visitor-Related Income

A World Heritage Site can be seen as a business enterprise: it generates cash at the site (admissions, books, souvenirs and food) and stimulates spending in the surrounding area. The site has an economic impact on nearby cities and villages, the region and the nation. Therefore, it is important to consider a site's economic potential and to put it in the service of the monument itself as well as the nation as a whole.

This chapter outlines different kinds of income opportunities and the ways to channel or reserve that income for specific site-related needs. Specific knowledge of the level and effects of visitor spending can help a site manager deal effectively with those elected and appointed government officials who have influence over the administration and financing of cultural sites.

Site Fees

It is necessary to set reasonable fees for site-related activities and plan for the allocation and use of this income. There should be a written policy on each of the following fees:

- **Admissions:**
  Identify and set the rate for different admission categories, i.e., individual, child, family, senior citizen, group, student, etc. For sites with large seasonal fluctuation in the number of visitors, a variation in admission fees for high and low tourist seasons may be appropriate. In developing countries, it may be appropriate to have a different admission-fee schedule for national citizens and international visitors. Review admission-fee schedules annually in relationship to site administrative expenses taking into account national economic trends such as inflation.
- **Licensing:**
  World Heritage Sites can generate income through licensing fees earned from the commercial production of such things as postcards, reproductions, facsimile documents, copies of art objects, recordings, etc. Fees should be set at a fair rate that takes into account the anticipated return to the business producing the product. The licensing fee, if possible, should be for a defined period of time and subject to renegotiation at specified intervals. It is desirable to earmark a high percentage, if not all, of the licensing income for use in maintaining the site and its collections.
- **Concessions:**
  For government-owned sites, concession agreements are usually negotiated directly with the central government office; the site administrator is seldom included in the discussions. Nor is it likely that the site's concession manager had anything to do with the negotiations. This often can cause problems on both sides. Be sure the site's interests are well represented in such negotiations. Any visitor service that is not, or cannot be, provided by the site administrator should have fee schedules included in the concession contract. Concessions may include food service, hotels or guest houses, tour guides, gifts and souvenir shops, transportation services, etc. It is desirable to have a minimum concession fee in the contract in addition to a predetermined percentage of the concessionaire's profits. Such contracts for visitor services should be for a specified time period and subject to regular review and renegotiation.
- **Rentals:**
  At large sites with an abundance of historic buildings, it may be appropriate to lease for compatible purposes those buildings that are not required for use in visitor interpretation. Such buildings also may be leased to site employees for housing. In some situations, it may be appropriate to make surplus buildings available for agricultural or commercial purposes, or for housing non-site related individuals. Rental income from leases should match prevailing market

rates in the area, with some possible adjustment for restrictions in use and access required by existing historical conditions. Leases should be for a specified time and subject to regular review and renegotiation.

When drawing up tenant leases, specify requirements for such things as maintenance of exterior and interior historic-building fabric, the use of outside spaces that are visible to the public, provision for private vehicles and the introduction of modern utility services. As was the case with concessions, restrict a high percentage of income from rental leases to ongoing maintenance, rehabilitation and restoration of the site's historic properties.

- **Permits:**
  The site administrator can issue special permits for a wide array of activities: to conduct archaeological research, to use open lands for agricultural purposes, to allow underground utility lines or systems to transverse the site, to permit hunting or fishing, to film commercial films or advertisements, and to copy archival reference materials. These special permits can carry variable fees depending on the scale and term of the specific activity. They should be set at a rate that realistically recognizes the potential profit to be made by the applicant. Such permits, too, should be issued for defined periods of time and be reviewed and renegotiated on a regular basis.

Use of Site Fees

Private owners of World Heritage Sites have wide latitude and discretion in deciding how to use income derived from the site. For government-owned sites, income will likely be subject to national policies. Most commonly, such income will go into the country's general revenue in the ministry of culture or department of finance. There are, however, examples where site income, either in its entirety or partially, stays at the site and/or the agency responsible for its administration. For example, Sri Lanka dedicates admission income from all its World Heritage Sites to an independent Central Cultural Fund that supports their administration, preservation and interpretation. In the United States, the National Park Service retains visitors' admission fees to heritage sites and rental income from surplus historical properties for preservation purposes.

Local Tourist Taxes

Public authorities may apply a range of taxes on tourists, covering transportation, airport departure, hotel stays, sales of goods and meals. Elected officials often find such taxes attractive because they provide much needed funds to local, state and national budgets without alienating voters by increasing their taxes. In some instances, a percentage of these taxes return for the maintenance and enhancement of tourist-related facilities and services. If tourist taxes escalate they can cause lower levels of visitation. If a location acquires a reputation for being overly expensive due to a high tax rate, tourists can, and will, select less expensive destinations. Site managers should monitor the local tourist-tax situation. First they should make every effort to retain as much as possible for site maintenance and second, they should challenge rates that threaten a site's attractiveness to tourists.

Effects of Related Visitor Spending

Because visitors spend only a small percentage of their total trip expenditure within the boundaries of a cultural site, it is vitally important for the administrator to recognize the broader economic impact of visitors within the community, region, state and country. Such information is important in dealings with local, state and national government agencies and with the broad spectrum of businesses dependent upon a site.

Site administrators should participate in local community service and business organizations such as the Rotary Club, Chamber of Commerce, etc. This can result in a potentially fruitful network of personal contacts.

For larger sites, it may be useful, from time to time, to commission outside economic impact studies to independently document how site visitor expenditures contribute to the local economy. Techniques exist for sampling both site visitors and for surveying businesses in the region. The national tourist office may conduct this research upon request.

Visitor expenditures to be documented include lodging and camping, restaurant food services, food and beverage market sales, personal and gift shopping, fuel and oil, automotive services, souvenir, craft and publication sales, as well as sales and value-added taxes at the local, state and national levels for all of the above.

Having command of this data helps a site administrator deal effectively with both elected and appointed government officials at all levels who have some influence over the administration or financing of cultural sites. Beyond demonstrating a site's economic benefit on and to its local setting, well-documented financial data help when negotiating with the local business and development community.

Chapter 6

Image and Marketing

Even though World Heritage Sites are by definition celebrated locations that command attention and draw visitors, it is still important for administrators to project the site's public image and target potential markets through publicity. This chapter reviews ways to create a public image and get exposure.

Professional marketing advice--often readily available from the business community and tourism boards--helps get critical information on the site into the hands of potential travelers all over the world. Marketing experts can help attract all the visitors the site can comfortably accommodate without turning it into a cheap carnival. They can help sell the site with dignity and balance scholarship with fame, purity with popularity.

Critical Imaging and Marketing Decisions

Many World Heritage Sites have been marketed for years as international tourism destinations. The tourism industry regards them as prime earners. Their owners, for their part, see them as sources of major income and need admission proceeds and other income to maintain these special sites.

The site administrator must address three important questions concerning marketing: 1) Are the site's true values and significance being projected in the current master plan and in previous marketing efforts?; 2) Is there a legitimate need for further, large-scale, commercial marketing?; and 3) If the site needs to be marketed, what is the controlling image to project to the public? (The site's fragility? Its quality? Its universal appeal?)

To answer the first question is a relatively simple matter. Check the nomination documents of the site and the World Heritage Committee's acceptance describing its values and significance. Look for terms such as "the tallest," "the oldest," "the last remaining," etc. These descriptions should help focus all promotional efforts. Popular legends may be associated with the site--Alexander the Great marched here, Cleopatra was born here, Gary Cooper made a movie here--but these should be treated as subsidiary stories.

The second question is also easily answered. The site may already have enough visitors, so the task is to give serious consideration to the effects of further commercial marketing. How many visitors can the site absorb? What route should tourists take to get there? Which types of tourists are most appropriate and desirable? Future marketing efforts may emphasize conservation and demonstrate methods of restoration.

To answer the third question above, the following topics need to be given careful and thoughtful consideration.

Creating and Projecting a Public Image

Each site has compelling characteristics that justify and explain its entry on the World Heritage List. This is its strongest tourism feature and an authoritative statement about it appeals to most visitors, so it should be included in national and international advertising. Furthermore, conservation matters can be a compelling attraction. Is there danger that the dome might collapse in an earthquake? Is there rising damp? Did the 19th-century restoration actually damage the foundation? Such questions and answers may be of special interest to visitors because it involves them in the care of what technically is part of the world's cultural patrimony shared by all.

At the same time, it is important to analyze the site for a deeper and more diverse range of interests. Are there many layers to the site's history? Is it significant to more than one religion or nation? Does it figure in a famous novel, poem or epic? Is it irrevocably associated with an era of history or a towering individual? Is it along a pilgrimage path or the route of explorers or conquerors? Did a particular artist or architect have a decisive influence there? These points of interest can extend and broaden a site's marketing opportunities.

Airlines, hotels and restaurants will have a wide range of stories to draw from to attract visitors. These features also provide much material for exhibits, publications and souvenirs. In no circumstance should stories be invented nor should part of the site's history be ignored or deliberately obscured. The truth is attractive, but deception is easily discovered and can ruin a site's reputation.

Marketing the Image

World Heritage Sites go through a rigorous nomination process that generally records their primary and secondary features. Be sure to communicate these qualities in a dignified and serious manner. Emphasize how the site's conservation constitutes an important gift and legacy to future generations. If expertise is not on staff, hire experienced and qualified marketing specialists to help.

It can be a complicated task to create a clear and concise public image. The site has international significance as well as national importance. It is situated in a particular environment; people live near it, next to it or even within it. Paramount is the protection of the site, and any plan must take into account all these factors. It is best that visitors arrive with a realistic understanding of the site and its condition so that they are prepared for both its magnificence as well as its problems--the stunning sunsets as well as the crowds, the unparalleled architecture as well as the noise of the marketplace. Subject to a site manager's guidance and armed with a clear vision, marketing professionals can develop over-all marketing concepts; craft a dignified and popular logo; place stories and information in magazines, newspapers, specialized newsletters and travel guides; and prepare press kits for researchers and writers. These professionals often are already working under some arrangement with the national tourist office, all the more reason for site management to reach out and establish a partnership or a special relationship with these tourism offices.

Legal Advice

Through the tourist office, site administrators can get legal advice on protecting the site's authorized logo and images. However, remember it can be unproductive to try to restrict the site to the degree that it keeps it from public media attention. It is important to have legal help in negotiating all media contracts, agreements and royalty rates.

Press Relations and the Press Kit

Travel magazines, newspaper travel sections and tourism industry newsletters are among the most important print media in which to market a site. Publishers, editors, reporters and writers should feel especially welcome at the site and have (preferably before they arrive) an attractive and informative press kit. The written and published results of such visits has the potential to reach a worldwide audience of millions. Ideally a press kit should, include: a site brochure; a one-or-two page fact sheet about the site's history and international significance; its priority conservation issues; a map showing the location of the site in relation to the surrounding area (or, for large sites, a simple site map); a listing of the times it is open to the public; one or two high-quality black and white photographs (with photographer credits and permission to reprint); a list of upcoming public events; and a sheet with complete names, addresses and telephone/fax numbers for those seeking further information. The contents of these press kits should be updated at least once a year.

Many writers will visit the site as part of a "familiarization (or fam) tour" organized by national tourism offices, airlines, or tour companies. Make sure the site is on the itinerary of any such tours.

Contact the organizers and make the necessary arrangements.

Television and radio staff are always on the look-out for feature or short subjects. It is important to cooperate with the electronic media but equally important not to let them over-run the site during production. Be sure to make all legal arrangements regarding credits, royalties and distribution.

Feature Books, Movies and Videos

One way to enhance the image and popularity of a site is to make available to visitors the books, movies and videotapes that feature the site. Often famous authors such as Agatha Christie, Somerset Maugham and Paul Theroux have used World Heritage Sites as settings in their travel books or fiction. Stock these books in the bookstore or gift shop, as well as lavish coffee-table picture books that contain dramatic and flattering photographs of the site. Because of their expense, these are best left to private publishers to produce. Many current and earlier films have included scenes shot at World Heritage Sites. If available on video cassette, they should be stocked for sale to visitors. Videos (VHS format, not BETA) on the site have become almost a basic requirement for any visitor attraction. These are commercially produced, and bids should be submitted to ensure getting the best product. Cassettes of television documentaries may be available and can be stocked if they are relevant.

International Museum Exhibits

The opportunity to participate in international traveling museum exhibitions can be a fruitful undertaking that projects a positive image of the site. The Festival of India and the Festival of Indonesia enjoyed enormous success in their tours of major museums in Europe, Japan and North America. Consisting of a number of exhibits and performances, the festival idea can elicit great interest in visiting the country's monuments and sites.

Such exhibitions are prestigious, serious and scholarly efforts undertaken at great expense. Although moving artwork always involves a risk, the objects displayed can be superb ambassadors and increase international exposure for the site. The licensing of the rights for reproductions of items included in such exhibitions --jewelry, small sculptures, images-- can also be an important source of revenue.

Postcards and Posters

Postcards and posters can be splendid, profitable and reliable marketing tools if they are well produced. It is not necessary to have a whole rack of choices. A few good ones will suffice. Get experienced and qualified firms to submit bids on producing postcards and posters. Have professionals help select the pieces that best present the image you want to project.

Travel and Trade Shows

Major international travel-trade shows are held annually in Berlin, London and Chicago. Numerous others are held at regional, national or state levels. These are buyer/seller trade shows where the national tourist office (NTO) presents the country's travel products to international tour organizers. These are important visitor-generating events and expensive to attend. Hence it is vital that administrators make sure their sites are well represented in the show by their respective NTOs. Even NTOs may find these shows expensive and often they join forces with a regional trade association (for instance, the Pacific Asia Travel Association, PATA) or political associations (such as the Association of Southeast Asian Nations, ASEAN) in booking exhibitor space at major shows.

A World Heritage Site can be a good selling point for the NTO, which should welcome the cooperation and input of the site's management. Make sure the NTO promotion properly represents the site's marketing image.

Commercial and Corporate Alliances

In some instances, it may be possible for a site to appropriately and advantageously join forces with the commercial marketing interests of a corporation. They should be asked to make a substantial financial donation, or provide needed equipment or supplies in exchange for permission to photograph their product on site, make a television commercial or film a movie. Again, it is important to have expert help in negotiating the best possible contract; which often can be an intricate affair with major financial implications.

Special Events

Anticipate demands to have the site host a variety of special events. Planned and conducted in a professional and sensitive manner, such special events can provide significant marketing opportunities. They have the potential of introducing the site to important and influential people -- political, diplomatic, corporate and private. Develop a plan that sets the limits of what the site can handle and is professionally acceptable. Some special events will be welcome, some must be rejected and others may be unavoidable. Certain religious festivals, national rallies or commemorative services may logically belong at the site. Planners may stage a fund-raising event to benefit the site or some other national cause; a special exhibition featuring new discoveries may be held at the site; or some entertainment entrepreneur may want to rent the site to stage an opera, a pageant or hold a reception for conventioneers.

Be in charge. Set limits. Have a plan. Analyze problems and opportunities for the site. Know ahead of time what is proper behavior and what would be inappropriate. Make sure guests also understand these same rules. Set visitor limits and enforce them. Try not to compromise in the face of local political and economic pressures.

Chapter 7

Recording and Analyzing Visitor Data

Statistical analysis of visitors can serve as a planning tool to help site managers forecast the future. The forms that travelers fill out enroute to their destinations provide a wealth of information. From visa applications, airport landing cards, customs declarations, hotel registrations, visitor surveys and other documents, tourism authorities are in a position to compile statistical profiles of proven and reliable accuracy. The British Travel Authority, for example, may know something about you just from these data. Are you one of the out-bound passengers who left Heathrow Airport in an economy class seat? Did you purchase your ticket from a travel agent? Is this your third trip to Asia and are you between 50 and 60 years old?

If you are, the Singapore Tourist Promotion Board knows what you will do after you land at Changi Airport. Based on in-bound statistics furnished by the United Kingdom, the board predicts you will stay three nights in a five-star hotel, spend S$148.00 on souvenirs, S$249.00 on food and purchase S$55 worth of duty-free items at the airport. You will take two half-day city tours, go to the zoo and the aviary and visit two museums!

By collecting data from visitors, site administrators can similarly predict whom to expect, what they will do and what they will most want out of their visit. This chapter discusses different kinds of data, collection techniques and analysis and their use by the management of World Heritage Sites.

On-Site Data Collection

Statistical information about on-site visitor activity measured over different time spans can be useful for planning purposes. A site administrator can collect data for the following time units:

- **Hourly:**
  How many visitors enter and leave the site each hour? The entrance and exit figures will provide an indication of what is the minimum, maximum and average time a visitor spends at the site. The figures will also indicate the busiest and slowest times. It may not be necessary to collect hourly data on a full-time basis. A periodic sample--for example, collecting data on Tuesday morning and Saturday afternoon--may suffice to provide the necessary data.
- **Daily:**
  How many visitors enter the site each day during the total number of hours it is open to the public? The hourly data can contribute to answering this question. These daily figures will serve as the basis for weekly, monthly and yearly statistics. The data will indicate the days of minimum, maximum and average visitation.
- **Weekly:**
  How many visitors enter the site each week during the total number of days it is open to the public? The daily data will translate into the weekly data. The weekly data, in turn, will serve as the basis for establishing visitor patterns over the course of the year. It is useful to know what are the weekly periods of lowest, highest and average visitation.
- **Monthly:**
  How many visitors enter the site each month during the total number of days and weeks it is open to the public? The daily and weekly data will translate into the monthly data. The monthly data will serve as the basis for establishing visitor patterns during tourism seasons. Which are the months of lowest, highest and average visitation?
- **Yearly:**
  How many visitors enter the site each year during the total number of months it is open to the

public? The weekly and monthly data will translate into the yearly data. The yearly data will serve as the basis for establishing visitor patterns over the course of a year. This yearly data is commonly used in public annual reports and serves as the most common public statistic for site visitation. Note how long tour operators allow for their stop at the site and relate fluctuations to bus or airline arrival and departure schedules.

Collection Techniques

There are several ways to collect visitor data with varying degrees of accuracy. Among the most common are:

- **Admission Tickets:**
  The numerical data provided by daily ticket sales serves as the most common form of data compilation where an entry fee is charged. Admission tickets should be numbered by type, i.e., adult, child, student, senior citizen, etc. The beginning and concluding stub numbers can easily provide an accurate count of daily visitation.
- **Automated Vehicular Traffic Counters:**
  For sites where visitors arrive commonly in vehicles, electronic traffic counters--commonly a sensor cable placed across the entrance roadway--can count the number of vehicles entering the site. This method can provide good data if the statistical average of the number of occupants per vehicle is determined at regular intervals.
- **Automated Visitor Counters:**
  An electric-eye counting device can record the number of people passing through an entrance gate. Accurate data depends upon making statistical adjustments for double-counting.
- **Turnstiles:**
  An entrance gate with a mechanical turnstile can maintain a count of the number of entries. This method can provide highly accurate data as long as movement proceeds in only one direction.
- **Hand-held Counters:**
  Guards or attendants stationed at entrance points can count the number of visitors through the use of hand-held mechanical counters. This data is reasonably accurate.
- **Visitor/Guest Registers:**
  Usually maintained at the entrance or exit, registers are signed by many visitors who like to leave a record of their presence at a site. This technique of recording visitors is most useful at small sites where visitors can be invited by a guide or hostess to sign the register. However, guests are under no obligation to sign, so this method can be unreliable. Still, the comments, names and addresses furnished can provide potentially more revealing information than mere numerical counting.
- **Parking Lot Surveys:**
  For sites with restricted parking lots, a periodic count of the automobiles and buses at given times can provide reasonably accurate data. The vehicular count has to be adjusted by determining and accounting for the average number of people per car.
- **Formal Visitor Surveys:**
  For sites that cannot collect and record visitor data using the above techniques, formal visitor surveys can be conducted according to a predetermined schedule. Such surveys might be done once or twice a month or every three months.

Off-Site Collections

Statistics collected off-site by other agencies can also be useful. By comparing data collected at the cultural site with broader statistical data from the area compiled by others, a manager can determine a number of visitor patterns, such as the percentage of foreign visitors coming to the region who visit the site. Chambers of commerce, highway departments, airports, railways, city tourist information centers and hospitality businesses (hotels, restaurants and local commercial tour authorities) often compile their own statistics.

Use of Collected Data

Data collected can be useful for a variety of purposes, including:

- **Staffing-needs projections:**
  The number of staff needed is directly related to the number of visitors who go to a site. A manager can plan how many staff are needed, when they are needed, and for how long.
- **Income projection:**
  By charting the flow of visitors to a site, a manager can also track an anticipated flow of income. When will income be heaviest? Lightest? Average?
- **Private funding proposals:**
  Potential donors, investors and contract service concessionaires will want to know recent, current and projected levels of visitation.
- **Public funding:**
  Departmental and ministerial fiscal officers will want to know the recent, current and projected numbers of visitors to the site. Site administrators need to have documented figures to maintain funding levels and/or justify increases.
- **Public relations:**
  Statistics are useful for press releases, promotions and announcements made throughout the year.
- **Special site promotions:**
  Visitor statistics can tell administrators when the fewest number of people will visit. During these times, special promotions can attract more visitors. Conversely, statistics can indicate when peak periods of arrivals occur, so that no public advertising or special promotions may be necessary.
- **Assessing Services and Infrastructure:**
  Knowledge of the fluctuation in the numbers of visitors also enables the site manager to assess the appropriateness of the site's existing services and infrastructure, and to plan for their maintenance and expansion.

Visitor Analysis

In addition to surveys of a strictly numerical nature, it is also important to collect qualitative data. Are visitors' expectations being met? Do they leave with a deeper knowledge of the site's significance? This information will enable the site's management team to evaluate the success of the didactic program and may prompt new ideas for interpretation, exhibitions and other activities currently absent from the site.

A simple, though sporadic method for collecting data can be in the form of "comment" and "suggestion" cards made available to the visitor at the end of the site visit. Pencils and a depository must be readily available for this method to succeed.

More sophisticated methods to collect qualitative data involve profiling visitors and interviewing them randomly. Seek professional assistance when developing the profile questionnaire in order to obtain meaningful polls.

Chapter 8

Visitors and the Local Population

When tourism moves away from the World Heritage Site itself into the local community, site managers need to ensure that both tourists and residents are prepared for the encounter. That is, visitors need education about residents and, vice versa, residents need understanding about tourists.

Sites have neighbors of different sorts. Historic urban areas encompass residents and businesses. In other locations, settlements may have grown up in, on or in close proximity to the historic site as, for example, at Borobodur in Indonesia. In still other situations, the local people, although living outside the World Heritage Site boundary, are themselves part of its living history, for example, the aborigines at Kakadu and at Ayers Rock in Australia. Local residents also may comprise part of the work force and be suppliers of services to the site; they may be worshippers, donors and political allies.

Often, the local population constitutes part of the destination product. Their outdoor markets, handicrafts, houses, cuisine, businesses, civic and religious centers, songs and dances may complement the site's didactic offerings and convey a special insight into its history and nature.

Thus a visit to a World Heritage Cultural Site can have two dimensions: first, to gain an understanding of a past culture and to perceive a link between its past, present and future; and second, to experience the local culture living around the site.

The opportunities for outside visitors to gather information on other cultures was restricted for centuries in many parts of the world. Travel to make these studies was a privilege limited to relatively few. The knowledge they sought was sometimes about culture--more often about politics. Most commonly early visitors sought to meet royalty or religious leaders. In the past, owners of what are now cultural sites did not want visitors on their grounds. Large-scale visitor access coincides with the explosion of tourism during the 19th century.

Today, more and more local communities are beginning to develop hostile or, at least, defensive attitudes toward visitors who are flooding their communities in increasing numbers. A World Heritage listing may bring a site international attention, but unless planners involve the local people, their "fame" may be considered a nuisance disrupting their previously quiet way of life.

This chapter considers some possible areas of contention between visitors and the local population. Although they may occur beyond the boundaries of a World Heritage Site, they must concern the site management team because of their effect on the visitors. Site staff need to prepare themselves to address public and private forums on these questions.

The Visitor Interface

Numbers of Visitors: Visitors use a great many facilities and services built mainly by and for the residents. Excessive numbers of visitors can strain these facilities and services, be it electricity, water, roads, parking places, or sanitation. The net result may be a decline in the permanent residents' quality of life.

- Vehicular Transportation:
  The circulation, loading and unloading, parking, and servicing of the visitors' vehicles--be they private automobiles, buses, taxis or boats--may be unwelcome intrusions that deny the local residents the freedom of movement, parking and services they need and expect. Noise and air pollution caused by increased tourist traffic may encourage some residents to move out of the area.

- **Business Conversions:**
  Basic, everyday businesses used by residents--food stores, cleaners, hardware stores, cobblers, etc.--may be forced out of their traditional locations by the increased rents charged for strictly visitor-related services such as souvenir shops, fast-food outlets, and up-scale gift and clothing shops.
- **Excessive Commercialization:**
  Where tourists congregate in large numbers, private businesses and commercial promoters seek to maximize their exposure through a combination of public advertising, billboards, signs, and perhaps loud-speakers. Large, poorly designed signs can be irritating and an eyesore. Concentrations of visitors also attract undesirable opportunists--unlicensed street vendors, entertainers or beggars.
- **Public Behavior:**
  Along with restaurants, bars, discos and other entertainment attractions comes antisocial public behavior--loud music, drunkenness, vandalism, littering, crime, indecency, and solicitation. Local residents shoulder the burden of increased expenditures for public safety and bear insults to their way of life. Sometimes the contrast between local residents and visitors may be confusing and dislocating, especially among local youth who attempt to emulate visitor's holiday behavior.

Residents may also come to resent the treatment they receive from visitors. Locals work out of necessity as waiters, chambermaids, porters and launderers. The sensitive site manager must be on a constant lookout for indications that social conflicts may be brewing. At the first sign of trouble, the site staff must take decisive steps to protect the traditional cultures with the same vigor and zeal that are spent in protecting all other cultural assets. They must stand ready to respond with whatever steps are necessary. This may include instituting educational programs that imbue the local community with a profound sense of pride in its traditions and allow them to make deliberate choices without the pressures that mass tourism sometimes unleashes.

Improving Economic Relations

Wherever possible and appropriate, local citizens should participate in and benefit from increased tourism. This can occur in a number of ways:

- **Employment:**
  The restoration and operation of a World Heritage Site is labor intensive. While scholars come from afar to plan and supervise the necessary conservation work, they expect a local labor force will be trained to do the field work. Of these some will eventually rise to take over curatorial, management and planning responsibilities. At Angkor in Cambodia, it is estimated that eventually 800-1,000 local people will be employed at the various monuments.

  And so it is with tourism. Hotels and restaurants also are labor intensive and provide many jobs that afford the possibility of upward-mobility. Owners conduct on-the-job training programs to improve the delivery of services and to keep up with their competition. Long-term career training and part-time or seasonal employment are common. Day labor is most apt to be used during construction periods. If there is an up-side for the residents of the nearby community, there may also be a down-side for the site administrator--tourism may increase the wage-scale for local labor at conservation projects.
- **Construction:**
  Most community social problems related to tourism tend to occur during the construction of new hotels, roads or other transportation facilities. This work is usually done by large national or international contractors who bring in their own crews. Seldom will the local community have enough skilled workers to work on a modern construction project. The presence of this imported, transient labor force can be disruptive to community values.

  Employment and construction problems can be managed best if they are anticipated. Unfortunately, many local officials do not prepare themselves adequately for these construction-related problems. The site administrator may play an important role by participating in advance preventive planning. In order to employ as many of the local labor force as possible on these construction sites, stipulations can be written into contracts, which also can require a certain amount of on-the-job-training to improve the community's skills-bank. Skills acquired during construction may transfer easily into permanent maintenance jobs on the site's grounds, buildings and mechanical equipment, as well as prepare for conservation work at the site.

The local community can also craft objects of local design and materials for guest rooms and public spaces. Carvers trained on the site may be able to get commissions from the developers to furnish decorative elements in the hotel. Pottery, weavings, paintings and metalwork can add to the interior decoration and form part of the inventory of retail shops. Again, the site administrator should be prepared to participate in efforts to get high quality work from the residents and the best price for their products.

- **Food Supplies:**
  Often, the presence of a tourism facility affects local patterns of food production and distribution. A hotel has to have a reliable daily supply of fresh fruits, vegetables, fish and meats. The community will probably have to reorganize its own traditions to do the job. As was learned by the community near a new resort in Malaysia, men can't just go fishing whenever they feel like it; someone has to go fishing every day to supply the "Catch of the Day" on the local hotel's menu.
- **Handicrafts:**
  If the site houses an official shop or concession, the administrator can provide an outlet for traditional products and help revive lost craft skills. Adapting a suitable building within the site to serve as an atelier for local artisans working in traditional styles may have the advantage of bringing them together in a central location for convenient interaction with the visitors. In lieu of rent, the site sponsor may receive a percentage of each item sold. A site's prestige may justify national distribution or international export of high-quality, signed or certifiably authentic handicrafts. Training programs, ways to purchase materials at wholesale prices and loans to improve the marketing of local products are other possibilities to explore.

Illegal Site Exploitation

The inscription of a cultural site on the World Heritage List brings with it international publicity. For sites with a rich archaeological heritage, this added attention may raise the site's profile with collectors and dealers. Objects associated with the site that are already in the marketplace may increase in value. Undoubtedly there will be pressure to find additional objects for sale to visitors. Sophisticated international smuggling rings find easy entry, especially where local incomes are marginal. Illegal excavation and pillaging can quickly move objects out of the site and into the international marketplace. In such instances, the site administrator must work closely with police and customs authorities to halt such activities. National governments can be pressured to ratify and implement international conventions formulated to thwart the illicit traffic in cultural property.

Creating Support for Tourism

Nurturing traditional handicrafts for sale in a site shop or concession can increase awareness and become a significant economic factor in the community. Ideally, residents will come to see themselves as community representatives --local hosts-- not just guides and taxi-drivers. The quality of their interaction with visitors can set a positive tone for the site visit. A welcoming attitude on the part of residents can make visitors feel secure.

It may be wise to form a local site advisory council to give focus to problems and offer a wide range of solutions. The site manager's role will be pivotal in the success of such an advisory council. He or she must be prepared to listen to the council's problems and suggestions and patiently explain conservation concerns or governmental regulations that affect the administration's decisions. Many advisory councils participate in site operations: they may act as volunteers to keep fresh flowers on an altar or a tomb, serve as guides during holidays and festivals and help raise money for some special project not included in the budget.

Contribution to the Public Purse

The site administrator must keep in mind the fact that an excessive number of tourists can create a drain on the local public purse. A solution may be to budget either a cash payment in lieu of taxes or some compensating adjustment to the community for its support and services. To ensure success, the site must fit into the community's daily life and be seen as a supportive good neighbor.

Involving Other Agencies

Many international agencies have programs and staff located in or around World Heritage Sites. These agencies include The World Bank, United Nations Development Program (UNDP), World Food Organization (WFO), World Health Organization (WHO) or the World Tourism Organization (WTO). These organizations work to promote community development using the same participation concepts outlined above. Site administrators should consider them natural partners in common efforts. For example, in the Sri Lanka Cultural Triangle project, a WFO food distribution allowance served as payment in lieu of wages for workers on some conservation sites. This kind of partnership can extend or add an appealing new perspective to foreign aid or relief programs.

WELCOMING VISITORS

Chapter 9

Moving Travelers to and from Sites

From the point of view of the travel industry, two 20th-century developments have irrevocably changed the world: the invention of the jet engine and explosive population growth. These events have ushered in an era of mass travel, in which more people than ever before can afford to travel to distant destinations.

As a result, World Heritage Sites are better known and more easily accessible. Yet along with increased popularity and more visitors comes a host of potential new problems. In most cases, a cultural site's standing walls, doorways, halls, pathways and grounds were not designed to accommodate huge numbers of people. Up until this century, for example, many temples were intended only for a handful of wandering scholars or pilgrims, while cities were visited primarily by mule trains carrying merchants and foreign goods.

The Influence and Opportunity of Air Travel

Air transport now provides the major mode of travel for long-haul arrivals and increasingly for domestic travelers as well. Most countries have designated one airport to serve as national hub, from which depart flights to the rest of the country. In this way, once remote areas have become accessible to travelers by smaller planes, charter flights and helicopters.

At many destinations, the rhythm of life is determined by the arrival and departure of airplanes: taxi drivers, restaurateurs, shopkeepers, guides and hoteliers plan their work schedules accordingly. (In some areas, the train or ship continues to set the tempo but mainly we live in an airplane age.)

Increasingly, airlines show passengers short films about their destination. These films often include information about airport procedures, customs regulations and traveler services. In addition, the films may include scenes highlighting some of the country's cultural attractions. Site managers seeking more visitors may wish to work with national tourist offices or the airline industry to be included in such films.

Airports have become focal points for visitor services, information, shopping and money exchange. Only a few airport managers make an active effort to present the best handicrafts and have pictures and brochures about the country's cultural attractions. Site managers should cultivate their interest. Frequently a wall painting or a large photomural in an airport can do much to publicize a site. The inclusion of brochures at the travel information counters, usually run by the NTO, is essential to attract visitors.

Certain sites attract air-charter flights in small planes or helicopters. This potentially popular mode of travel can have detrimental effects, but should not be ignored. Likely civil safety regulations govern such operations, so site managers would be wise to enter into discussions with this branch of the airline industry to protect their sites.

Ground Transportation

In many regions, the railroad continues to play an important role, especially for domestic travelers. Like airports, train stations have information counters and offer potential installation spaces for paintings or photomurals. It is important that a site's location be clearly indicated on all maps distributed or displayed.

In many cities, street-car, bus and subway systems are connected to airports and train stations. Each of these systems usually has a contract agency that handles advertising. They usually are glad to include some free institutional ad spaces. This is where the marketing officials at the NTO or their advertising agency can best help a site manager to work with the contract firm to get the most effective design and convey the right message to potential visitors.

Taxi drivers are usually among the first local residents with whom the visitor converses. They, therefore, should be cultivated as friends. Like tour bus drivers, they should be knowledgeable about the site and have accurate information. Many public transportation systems have prepared brochures of packaged tours along their routes. These often help travelers get access to otherwise remote sites.

Special Site Transportation Systems

Special types of transportation--horse-drawn carts, funiculars, boats, electric golf-carts and small trams--reduce exhaust fumes and noise as well as lessen wear and tear on the site. In addition to assisting in crowd control, they can become attractions themselves, admired by visitors for their picturesque qualities.

To operate efficiently, such transportation systems should have designated waiting and boarding areas. Local governments must maintain a licensing system, control the number of operators, and monitor the quality of service. Each mode of transport poses its own set of challenges: For example, in the case of horse-drawn vehicles, it is necessary to provide for sanitary clean-up and disposal and the humane treatment of the animals.

Where horses or donkeys are used to move visitors in and out of a site, the effect of animal hooves on trails and road surfaces needs to be considered. Moreover, such animal transports in hot and dry climates can raise large amounts of dust, affecting both tourists and monuments.

Tour Buses

Tour bus operators want satisfied customers. They often give a mini-lecture or show videos on the bus ride to the site. Be sure that their guides are informed about its history, as well as its rules and regulations. Know in advance how long bus groups will spend at the site. Specify locations for loading, unloading and parking, and institute an efficient ticketing procedure for group visits. Placement of the gift shop along the route leading back to the buses can help in moving large numbers of people through sites with minimal damage or discomfort.

Taxi Stand

If there is a taxi stand, it should be unobtrusive but clearly marked, provide for all-weather pick-up and drop-off, display a map of the city and post the official fares.

Independent Transportation

Provision must be made for private automobiles, motorcycles and bicycles. Because visitors who arrive independently will not have had the benefit of a guide to prepare them for the visit, directional signs to ticket kiosks, entry gates, toilets, shops and restaurants are necessary for this type of visitor.

Some general principles for handling private vehicles are:

- Beginning at some distance from the site, install graphically effective directional signs to help drivers locate the site;
- Design directional signs, street and road patterns and even pavement colors to help guide

vehicles;

- Locate a convenient passenger drop-off and pick-up a reasonable distance from the entrance, providing for the needs of elderly and visitors with disabilities;
- Encourage visitors to leave their vehicles outside the site. Discourage visitors experiencing the site from behind the steering wheel of a vehicle;
- Do not allow large concentrations of parked vehicles to physically and aesthetically intrude on the historic site. In the case of an urban historic zone, it may be necessary to provide for a parking garage well outside the protected zone.
- At a large metropolitan site, a shuttle bus service can carry visitors to and from remote parking lots. In an undeveloped rural environment, it may be advisable to screen the parking lot to prevent it from intruding upon and marring the historic scene;
- Charge a separate fee for parking, if necessary;
- Where large parking facilities are part of the site's operation, provide for security patrols to prevent thefts of vehicles and break-ins. At sites with great fluctuations in visitation from high to low seasons, consider creating a permanent parking area and an overflow lot;
- Locate separate staff parking close to the site.

Boats

When visitors arrive by boat, the site manager has an opportunity to take advantage of the time spent aboard to familiarize the passengers with the site and provide a psychological break between departure and arrival. Guides on board can tell the story of the site, provide printed information and explain conservation efforts. They can review the rules of the site and be available to answer questions. Private boats should not be allowed to dock without paying a fee, and their crews should include guides licensed by the site manager.

Access for Visitors with Disabilities

Access for persons with disabilities has now become a universal expectation. Every effort should be made to provide the maximum possible access for every visitor. This does not, however, mean that your site's authenticity has to be physically damaged to solve this problem. It may well be that handicapped access will be impossible at some historic sites--entire sites or major parts thereof. There may be ancient steps, basements, caves or unpaved paths. This situation can be accepted, but it must also be explained upon arrival. In some cases, it may be possible to provide alternatives such as books, videos or slide-shows.

Some countries are still preparing universal access legislation. It is important that your government ministry participate in these deliberations so that new laws do not damage historic sites through insensitive requirements.

Chapter 10

Visitor Amenities and Services

Visitor satisfaction comes from thoughtful planning; problems must be anticipated and solved ahead of time. There are two aspects of this process: 1) amenities--the careful, subtle, gracious extra details that give the visitor a heightened sense of friendship, pleasure and joy; and 2) services--meeting the minimal expectations of any visitor to find food, toilets, water, shops, telephones, check room, etc.

Amenities may be defined as the attempt to solve problems with style. This might include the graphic design of a sign, the selection of trees, shrubs and flowers, the alignment of paths, the placement of lamps, benches and chairs. All sites need a parking lot, but it needn't be just a sheet of asphalt.

Site administrators manage renowned historic sites that most probably had some kind of amenity: trees, paved paths, entrance portals, a garden or a pond and running water. Recapturing or restoring these original landscape amenities can add to the richness of the visitor's experience.

This is another situation where it is important to reach out to other professionals to get help and advice. Research on the original amenities has progressed dramatically through archaeological excavations and study of early diaries and archival records. If scholars cannot say exactly what a site originally looked like, they can explain what kind of landscape architecture prevailed in the region during different historical periods.

Like visitor services discussed below, some amenities will be modern intrusions: lights, signs, benches and drinking fountains. Contemporary trees and shrubs can also be used in the area, but this should be a professional, not a casual decision; nothing should suggest that they were part of the historical fabric. There should be a sense of appropriateness to whatever is introduced.

Accommodations

Visitors to cultural sites require the provision of a range of accommodations, from luxury hotels to campgrounds. The type of cultural site being administered--whether a historic city, a single urban monument, a palace complex or an archaeological site--requires that planners consider a variety of factors before formulating policies and practices in regard to accommodating visitors on overnight stays.

Unless a site is remote and difficult to travel to, it is generally advisable to leave all matters concerning hotels, guest houses, hostels and camping facilities to the private sector or relevant government agencies. These structures should be located away from the site. Planning, financing, developing, operating and maintaining such facilities within the site can be a complex, expensive, distracting and time-consuming administrative responsibility.

Hotels

Nevertheless, the decision might be made to provide hotel accommodations on site. The size of any such hotel will have to be determined by the number of visitors likely to seek accommodations and the capacity of the site to support such a facility. Hotel location and design need careful attention when formulating the site's master plan. This is especially important not only in aesthetic terms but also in terms of access: consider all the many types of vehicles that must go to and from the building. It is likely that any such hotel will be subject to thorough review and approval by government bodies responsible for the site's protection.

Once concerns for appropriateness are met, it is then important that within those limits, the best possible hotel be built--one that not just houses guests but contributes to the value of their visit. The ideal hotel should be unobtrusive but supply views of the monument from its lobby, bars, restaurants, terraces and guest rooms.

It may be appropriate to consider the adaptive use of a historic building as a hotel facility. The design of such a facility should be undertaken within the framework of a carefully drawn set of architectural standards and guidelines in order to protect, preserve and respect the significant architectural features of the building(s). Both the architects and building contractors selected for such work should be carefully screened and their prior experience given careful consideration and investigation.

If a new building is required, exercise caution that its program is not only functional but also compatible with its historic environment. It should be designed in a manner so as not to intrude upon or distract from the visitor's experience of the site. Particularly important are the siting, height, massing, exterior materials, their color and texture, and surrounding landscape treatment.

It is imperative that the site administrator draw up precise and legally sound contracts and leases for any privately developed and operated facilities. These documents should cover all aspects of accommodation services--i.e., schedules of operation, selection and approval of all furnishings and decor, operational staffing standards, maintenance standards, advertising and promotion provisions, public health and safety standards, insurance and liability provisions, room rates, profit percentages between concessionaire and site administration, and termination provisions. Consultation with a contracts lawyer is highly recommended.

An on-site hotel must be more than just a functional facility. Beside being appropriate, it should incorporate the best advice from experienced planners, hotel architects and landscape designers to assure maximum visitor satisfaction. In numerous game lodges in wildlife parks, lodge buildings have also become viewing platforms for observation and photography. The hotel itself has become part of the park experience. The same can apply to a cultural site where the hotel adds to the entire experience, facilitates and enhances it. For example, travelers to Macchu Picchu in Peru who stay in the modest hotel on-site have the opportunity to see the Inca site at dawn, an unforgettable experience unavailable to those traveling by train and bus from Cuzco.

In urban historic zones, increased international and domestic visitation can often create a situation where developers acquire residential and commercial properties for conversion into hotels and guest houses. If proper zoning controls are not in place, such unrestricted construction can have a dramatic effect on the character of the historic area. When traditional businesses and long-time residents have to relocate to make room for tourist enterprises, this may negatively affect relations between the local population and visitors. A limit should be established on the total number of hotel accommodations that will be permitted within the historic zone. In some situations, developers have demolished actual historic buildings to be replaced by new hotels designed in a historical style. This is not a development to be encouraged within or near a World Heritage Site.

Guest Houses and Hostels

Smaller and less heavily visited sites may accommodate visitors in small-scale guest houses or hostels. The same overall comments made in regard to hotels apply to guest houses and hostels. The same precautions must be observed while the same opportunities for creative, memorable facilities exists.

Camping

In many countries, a high percentage of visitors prefer to camp, either alone, with their family or in a group. At remote sites camping may be the only option. Determine the maximum number of campsites allowed and then rigidly adhere to it by using an advance-reservation system.

Camping facilities that can accommodate automobiles, trailers and large mobile touring vans require sophisticated services such as gasoline, oil and other automotive facilities, sewage disposal hook-ups for vehicle systems and public toilets, showers and laundry facilities. To operate in an environmentally safe manner, these require a proper water supply and a sewage disposal system. Such campsites might also require small-scale grocery stores and security patrols.

Public Services

For a cultural site to welcome visitors, the following services are mandatory in order to function in an enjoyable, safe and sanitary manner:

Potable Drinking Water

Public drinking fountains, dispensing potable water, should be readily available to visitors in the vicinity of the site entrance(s), at food service facilities and near public toilets. Water supplies should be checked on a regular basis by the public health authorities to ensure its safety. Fountains should be clearly identified using standard international graphic symbols.

Toilets

An adequate number of men’s and women's toilet facilities should be available to visitors. In many instances their number will be determined by local building regulations. They should generally be located near the entrance(s), eateries and, at large sites, interspersed at convenient locations. Toilets can be located in historical structures that lend themselves to such adaptive use. Public toilets should be clearly identified using standard international graphic symbols. In many countries visitors are expected to pay a small fee for the use of these facilities. This helps pay for their maintenance.

The location and construction of sewers, septic tanks, and drainage fields require careful consideration. Sewers should always be covered and built of a highly durable material. They should be designed for ease of access in order to be serviced and maintained. Where a connection to a public sewage treatment facility is not possible, the necessary septic tanks and drainage fields should be located in an area not subject to visitor use, either regular or temporary. Their potential impact on the existing water table needs to be considered. It is especially important not to permit any activity that might result in breakage or blockage of the drainage field system. For example, do not use a septic drainage field as a temporary parking lot for a special event. Septic tanks need to be located so that service trucks can have easy access for pumping and cleaning.

Food Service

When a site offers meals to visitors, they may be provided either by staff or an outside food concessionaire. A portion of the operation might be appropriately developed to be part of the historical interpretation of the site, so that servers wait on customers in costumes that replicate some phase of the history of the site. The menu might also reflect the food-ways of the site’s inhabitants.

Options range from stands dispensing beverages and snacks to a full-service restaurant. All will have to meet local health and sanitation requirements and be subject to regular inspection by the governing public authorities. The location of such facilities should be convenient for the visitor and accessible by staff and service vehicles making deliveries. In sites with a surplus of unused spaces within historical buildings, it may be appropriate to adapt them for food service uses. The architectural design and interior decoration should respect the overall architectural character of the building and site. Finally, adaptive use requires particular attention to the installation and maintenance of fire detection and suppression systems in the kitchen areas.

If a commercial firm is to provide food services, a carefully drawn legal contract is required between the site administrator and the contractor. The contract should cover all aspects of the food-service operation, i.e., hours of operation, menu selection, serving utensils, furnishings and decor, owner-access to the facilities, adherence to governing health and sanitary codes, pricing, profits to the contractor and owner, liability coverage, insurance, and termination provisions.

Public Telephones

Visitors should have access to public pay telephones. Generally they should be located at the entrance(s) and near dining and toilet facilities. Instructions for their use should be in the major languages spoken by most of the site's visitors, and local telephone directories should be made available. Post near the telephone frequently called numbers such as taxi service. Some countries use illustrations of their cultural heritage sites on the covers of telephone directories. This may be an effective way of promoting a site to a wide market of both local residents and foreigners.

Emergency Medical Service

Basic emergency medical kits should be available at the site's administrative headquarters. For larger sites, these kits might be appropriately distributed at several locations throughout the site. Designated staff should have training in emergency first-aid procedures, which is often available from local chapters of the Red Cross or public emergency services. Telephone numbers of fire, police, rescue and medical services should be posted at the administrative headquarters and entrance gates.

Postal

If a site gets enough visitors, it may be desirable to have a small postal station to sell stamps and accept the posting of mail. This facility should be conveniently located near the main entrance or in proximity to the gift and sales shops. The facility must be accessible for mail trucks. Beyond meeting the standard requirements of the nation's postal service, the facility should respect the site's historical character.

Trash Collection

To prevent litter, a site should have sufficient numbers of well-designed, durable and conveniently placed trash receptacles throughout the site. Label them with the accepted international symbol for trash and, if necessary, in the most commonly used visitor languages. They should not carry advertising; often companies might offer to pay for the cost of these receptacles if they have the exclusive right to advertise their product or service on them. Such advertising is inappropriate and takes away from the visitor experience. Trash receptacles should complement their surroundings and be designed to discourage animals and rodents from gaining access. They should be located to allow easy access by small service vehicles.

Where site visitation is high, such as at Egypt's pyramids, a cleaning crew may be needed to regularly pick up trash. Their presence reminds visitors that they should not litter. With training, the cleaning crew can also support the guide and security efforts.

A site manager may wish to negotiate a contract with an outside food concessionaire that includes clean-up as part of the terms.

Garbage Removal and Disposal

A site should have one or more central garbage collection points located away from visitors and screened by suitably designed fences or landscape features such as hedges or trees. Large garbage trucks must be able to gain access to the site without disruption to the visitors. Such services may be provided either by public trash collection vehicles or those of a private contractor.

For sites generating large quantities of garbage, use covered metal containers designed specifically for this purpose. Because accumulated trash invariably attracts rodents and other pests, regular extermination efforts may be required. But it is safer and cheaper to control rodents through elimination of their food supply by adopting and enforcing stringent sanitary conditions.

Commercial Retailing

Most tourists come to a cultural site expecting to purchase something related to their visit. Decisions on commercial products at a cultural site--what is sold, who sells it, at what price and what happens to the profits are all important concerns.

A concentration of visitors acts as a magnet for vendors of all sorts. A policy needs to be established that controls those wishing to sell goods at the site. If they are forbidden access to the site, the site administrator should work with local authorities to control where vendors can set up outside the site's boundaries. Lack of controls can result in unattractive conditions at the site's major entrances.

If vendors are allowed on the site, experience shows that the site administrator must license them to ensure control over their numbers, merchandise sold, time of operation, term of licensure, access fee, and profit sharing. The total number of individual vendors should be limited. Where competition is high, a lottery may be necessary. They should operate only within carefully designated zones. All merchandise sold should be reviewed by the site administrator as to their appropriateness and price. If vehicles are allowed--moveable vans or wagons and/or temporary stalls--their design should be approved before it is allowed onto the site. Hours of operation need to be set. Anyone operating within site boundaries should be expected to share some predetermined percentage of profits with the site administration. This can be done in varying ways: as a percentage of sales reported and taken on a daily, weekly or monthly basis; as a licensure fee required on a daily, weekly, monthly or annual basis; and as a competitive bid fee for the right to sell within the site for a specified time period.

Ticketing

Sites that charge an entrance fee need to have a ticketing facility--one at the main entrance gate and the other in an office for advance-group ticket sales.

Ticket prices should be clearly posted both at the point of sale and at a prominent location where just-arriving visitors can study the pricing structure and make individual decisions on what they wish to purchase. This is especially important where optional tours are offered with varying charges. The local language and local currency should be used. Globally, English has become the language of international tourism, but do what seems appropriate and efficient at your site.

Most ticketing booths are located at the site's entrance(s). They should be clearly visible and well marked for all arriving visitors. They may be accommodated within a historic building that lends itself to adaptive use, such as a visitor-receiving facility. The sale of admission tickets, books and souvenirs should ideally be separated so as to reduce confusing circulation patterns.

Ticketing facilities should be designed to respect the site's architectural character and have adequate security to protect the ticket-sellers, the supply of tickets and the cash receipts. Ideally, the purchaser should be protected from inclement weather.

At sites that are large or without a complete array of visitor facilities, the ticketing operation should allow visitors to exit and re-enter during the same day. This can be accommodated by having tickets with multiple stubs or stamping the backs of visitors' hands.

Managers may decide to divide the site into several distinguishable units. Such a system can require visitors to purchase tickets for different components of the site. This distributes visitors to different regions of the site rather than having them concentrate at just the prime locations.

Group tour visitors should not be expected to stand in long lines to purchase tickets. Their tickets should be handed out in advance of their arrival.

High and Low Season Visitation

Most sites will experience significant variations in the number of visitors during the course of the year. This will be influenced by such factors as prevailing weather conditions, school holiday periods and dates of religious festivals. Advanced planning should carefully estimate this variation in numbers because it has a major impact on the design of various facilities required to accommodate visitors--bus and auto drop-off spaces and parking, toilet facilities, etc. After an initial period of operation, visitation patterns should be studied for any possible effects on site planning, programming, staffing and budgeting.

Photography Policies

It is advisable to have written policies governing the use of photographic equipment at a site and to distinguish between the policies applicable to the general public and those that apply to commercial photographers. The policies relating to the general public should be posted in a highly visible location at the entrance. If there are areas where photography is prohibited, post the notices prominently and explain the reasons clearly. The policies that apply to commercial photographers should be available in written form.

In general, be positive about visitor photography. If managed right, snapshots and home movies can be great boosts for the country and site. The admission price should include the use of cameras. Use of hand-held personal film and video cameras can usually be allowed on all publicly accessible exterior portions of the site. Depending on the characteristics of a site and local customs, there is no reason to restrict the use of cameras within the interiors of historic buildings. It is important not to allow the use of flash units and video camera lights within a historic building. The repeated exposure of materials to high-intensity lights can be damaging.

There was a time when it was thought that amateur photography competed with the sale of postcards and souvenir books; retailers no longer believe this to be true. Moreover, the sale of film and disposable cameras can be an important source of revenue.

Use of tripods and light stands by visitors should not be permitted inside historical structures because their use can damage both finishes and furnishings. It also interferes with visitor circulation.

Commercial Photographers

Always retain the reproduction rights for commercial use of photographs taken from publicly restricted portions of the site. Establish a schedule of permit fees for this purpose. Contractual arrangements might also include the right of the site to use commercial photographs without the payment of a fee.

Restrict use of specialized equipment to officially licensed, or sanctioned, commercial photographers. A member of the administrative staff should supervise the shoot at all times. The permit or contract allowing such commercial use should always have a provision or clause that makes the photographer responsible for any damage to objects or furnishings.

World Heritage Sites may often be proposed as filming sites by major national and international movie production companies. Have a formal written policy concerning such commercial undertakings. The policy and contracts should be carefully drawn to ensure that management remains in control of all aspects of the use of the site for productions. Contracts should include the right to prior review of the movie script before granting access, to define areas and times of access, to control the placement and use of all production equipment, to protect against damage to all site features and contents, to make provision for payment in the event of any damage, to collect fees for the use of the site and to require public credit and acknowledgment in the final product.

Chapter 11

Site Interpretation and Visitor Education

Successful interpretation and effective presentation of a cultural site begin with a vision and a plan, one that takes as its starting point a consideration of the visitors. Who are they? What are they looking for? What does management want them to see and learn and enjoy? The plan must then specifically describe all interpretative elements--written materials, visual and graphic displays, exhibits, sensory and hands-on opportunities. The plan must also aim to communicate particular themes and concepts that in the opinion of site administrators and staff convey the essence of the site's significance.

Visitor Types

Every site attracts particular kinds of visitors. They may have different interests, may speak different languages, and have different reasons for visiting the site. Some are on a patriotic journey, others are on pilgrimage. Some come out of curiosity, others to place a check-mark on a personal list of travel adventures. Some come out of a lifelong wish, others come to be off the beaten track. People from every walk of life will visit the site. For the purpose of interpretation and education, it is useful to think of visitors according to the following categories:

- **The Scholar Visitor:**
  Some visitors will come well prepared and familiar with the history of the site. They know prior to arriving many of the site's features and those attractions they especially want to experience first-hand. For this audience the primary responsibility is to make their visit as pleasant, easy and informative as possible. They will not want to be rushed, but visit the site at their own pace on their own rather than with an organized group. They may spend extended periods of time studying and photographing a few features of the site. They will be interested in examining and purchasing specialized publications concerning the site that may not be available elsewhere. They will be knowledgeable (and possibly critical) of what is being offered for public interpretation. If they do employ a guide, they will expect a high degree of expertise.
- **The General Visitor:**
  Some visitors will come because they have heard about the site or read a little about it in a tour book, but generally they have scant prior knowledge. They seek a comprehensive presentation of the site that provides a general understanding of its international, national and local historical significance. This type of visitor constitutes a major target audience of the interpretative program. They should leave believing that they have had an informative visit, one that they will want to pass on to their friends and acquaintances who may then wish to visit the site.
- **Students:**
  The site is likely to be visited by many students. Depending on their educational level, a separate interpretative program may be required for them. The program must focus on a few essential lessons, provide comprehensible written materials, and be kept to a length that will not tire them or tax their capacity to concentrate. So as not to disturb other visitors, school groups can be scheduled separately or introduced to the site at an educational center designated for their use.
- **The Reluctant Visitor:**
  A small segment of visitors will be people who have been brought to the site as part of a package tour or group outing. They come with little if any advance understanding of the site and are often there just because this is where the bus brought them. They are often more interested in the amenities--where to get something to drink, where the toilets are, where to sit down and where the gift shop is. They should be made to feel welcome and encouraged to experience the site however they wish. Be patient, don't be overly concerned that do not show great interest in what the site has to offer; much may rub off on them through osmosis without them being aware of it.

Reception and Visitor Orientation Center

As a basic element, the site should have a visitor reception and orientation center. Here the visitor first stops to purchase an admission ticket, secure a guidebook and brochure and view an introductory exhibit. For larger, heavily visited sites, an audio-visual program shown on a regular basis might also be made available. When the visitor leaves the center, he or she should have a basic understanding of the site's significance, its size and what options it offers visitors in terms of experiencing the site. For large sites, such as an urban historical district or a large battlefield, more than one visitor reception area may be needed.

Exhibits intended to explain specific features of a site usually are most effectively located near them and away from the main entrance. For large sites with widely distributed points of interest, trail-side exhibit panels may be an effective means of interpretation. These panels are usually modest in size (not to distract attention from the main attraction, the site itself) and should be designed to withstand inclement weather and be vandalism resistant.

Printed Information

Advertisements: Not all World Heritage Sites need to advertise. Some attractions are so well known that the problem is not enough but too many visitors. For less familiar destinations, ads in travel magazines, newspapers, trade journals, and on radio and television (and now a "home page" on the World Wide Web, part of the global Internet computer network) are ways for visitors initially to learn about the site and spark interest in visiting it. Advertisements are often the first step in the visitor's interpretative experience. They need to be graphically appealing, historically informative, and succinct. Don't hesitate to ask the advice of advertising experts.

For sites that can afford it, an annual advertising campaign can be an important way to reach potential audiences. However, it is critical to retain close control over what the advertising presents to the public. This can be accomplished by getting involved with the advertising agency at key times throughout the development and production of the program--not just at the beginning. The message reaching the potential visitor through print, sound or visual images needs to be of high quality, clear, consistent and positive.

In some instances, public and privately owned sites may be able to secure donated or discounted services from leading advertising firms as part of their public service program. Magazine and newspaper editors may at times be willing to run prepared advertisements to fill unsold advertising space in their publications. Collaborative advertising campaigns can also be developed in conjunction with local chambers of commerce, national, regional or city tourist offices, major local hotels and national airlines.

- **Brochures:**
  A brochure, preferably illustrated, is a basic necessity for any site. At sites charging an admission fee, the cost of the brochure should be built into the price of the ticket. For sites with no admission fee, it can either be distributed free or sold for a nominal charge. Its content should include basic historical information, the schedule of the site's operation, and the visitor services available. It should be illustrated with a good map and a few representative photographs or drawings. It should be available in the local language, in English and in other languages frequently spoken by visitors. It should be designed to easily fold into a shape that fits in a pocket or purse and be easy to use.

- **Guidebooks:**
  In addition to the basic brochure, a more comprehensive, illustrated guidebook to the site should be available for purchase. It should be sold at a location that all visitors must pass entering the site. Again, it should be available in the local language, English and the language(s) of the most frequent visitors. The preparation, publication and sale of such guides may result from a joint

venture between the site and a commercial publisher. The site is in a position to provide the necessary historical data, photographs, and illustrations. The publisher is in a position to provide the writing, editing, design, production, and marketing skills.

- **Books:**
  Visitors who enjoyed their time spent at a site may want to purchase one or more books before leaving. They want to learn more about it, take something home to remind them of their visit or give something to a friend or relative. A range of books should be available of different types: (historical, pictorial, interpretive), prices (inexpensive to expensive) and reading level (child to adult, general public to scholar). A well-designed display of these books in a gift shop, easily available to both arriving and departing visitors, is an important educational service. Two things to remember: most children's books are purchased by adults; and don't stock too large an inventory--specialize in books that emphasize the site.
- **Maps:**
  Just as it is important to have the site identified on standard national, state and regional highway maps, make available good location maps for the visitors. People like to know where they are and where they are going in relation to the total site. A large, easily readable, well-illustrated map posted at the entrance is a must. Smaller maps and building floor plans placed at key locations around the site are also important. For an urban historic district, large maps should be placed at key public gathering places. Each map, in addition to depicting the entire district, should highlight the most significant buildings and sites within the immediate area. The site administrator should work with all local public transportation authorities--railways, metros, streetcar, and bus companies--to ensure that the maps displayed both in transport vehicles and at the station clearly indicate the stops where visitors should get off for the site.

Signage

Well-designed and strategically placed signs serve an important role in any site's overall interpretative program. If at all possible, a readily comprehensible logo unique to the site should be developed for use in conjunction with the World Heritage logo. It should be used on all signs, maps and printed materials related to the site. Signage should be part of the comprehensive interpretative plan and care given to the size, design, graphic treatment, color and materials used in signs.

The following types of signs need to be considered. It is best to use internationally recognizable symbols and colors wherever possible.

- **Highway Directional:**
  Work with local transportation authorities to develop a signage system that provides general directions to the site. In some instances, state or national highway authorities have design standards governing such signs and exercise rigid control over their placement. For visitors leaving a site, make sure to provide directional signs to route them efficiently back to the hotel or stop. Where commercial highway advertising is allowed, a number of distinctive signs, often indicating the distance to the site, can be a welcome visitor service. Periodically check to see that all signs are well maintained.
- **Signs Around and On Site:**
  As visitors approach the site, it is important that signs direct them to where you want them to go. Usually this will be the main entrance and the parking facilities. Directional signs at the entrance should be simple and direct so as to be easily comprehended from a moving vehicle. In those instances where public security may be an issue, signs may be required in the parking lots to warn visitors that the site administration is not responsible for articles left unattended in parked vehicles. Directional signs should also indicate special areas where trucks, vans and buses should go. In urban areas, signs may also be required to limit parking time so as not to have the parking area used by local residents and employees. Within the site, directional signs should be designed and placed to provide the visitor with clear directions on how to follow the visitor circulation

path(s), to locate public services and amenities and to locate the exit. At major interpretative points, signs can provide the visitor with basic information. All of these need to be sensitively designed and placed so that they do not intrude on photographs of the historic scene, vistas or the building character. Signs need to be fabricated and mounted in such a way as to be both weatherproof and vandal resistant. Felt pens and spray-paint have become universal threats to monuments. The damage that they create can be frighteningly permanent. Removing them is often itself destructive to patina and materials. There is no fool-proof protection, but visible and attentive on-site security can help reduce the problem.

- **Emergency Signs:**
  For buildings, local regulatory codes may require the placement of lighted signs to direct visitors to emergency exits. Signs should clearly identify the location of emergency fire-fighting equipment.

Exhibits

Exhibits incorporating a combination of text, graphics, objects, models, dioramas and audio-visual elements, can add greatly to the visitor's understanding of the site. The planning, design, fabrication and installation of exhibits is best left to professional exhibit designers. Should these services not be available within the site's organization, care should be taken in selecting outside contractors. What will be produced will likely have a long life, be seen by thousands of national and international visitors and be an expensive undertaking. It is, therefore, important to carefully interview contractors, review examples of prior work and check their references.

It is important that site administrators and staff carefully delineate through the exhibit program the essential lessons and themes of the site. Everything that is known cannot be shared with visitors. The task is to define and limit the interpretative effort to the most significant and interesting themes and points. A master exhibit plan for the whole site, even if it cannot be implemented all at the same time, is an important planning tool.

Narrated Slide Presentation

An automated slide projection system, with an accompanying narrative audio tape, provides one of the least expensive and most flexible audio-visual tools. The program can be easily altered or updated. Introductory shows should be shown near the main entrance in a properly designed space. The space should be reasonably darkened, properly ventilated and have simple seating. The length of the show should not exceed five minutes.

Video Tape Presentation

Video presentations are becoming more widespread and replacing slide presentations in many places. Video production requires the services of a company that can produce both the desired script and visual images and then edit them into an interesting presentation. While being more durable than a slide presentation, video is more expensive and is less easily updated or revised. Because of the widespread use of video tapes, and their growing popularity as a site souvenir, tapes can be sold to visitors to help recoup the cost of their production. Presentations can be highly flexible in length of time but most are 25-30 minutes. Their length may require a small theater or a separate viewing space.

Film

Good for large and heavily visited sites, motion pictures are expensive to write, film, narrate, edit and produce. They require sophisticated equipment and personnel to be shown on a regular basis. For maximum visitor effect, films require proper screening rooms with good sight lines and acoustics. Film can be used in a highly productive way by national tourist offices around the world. For multipurpose use, i.e., at the site and for promotional use away from the site (especially television), films should not exceed 25 minutes.

Rental Tape-Recorded Tours

A normal amenity at many museum exhibits, rental audio tapes are becoming more popular at cultural heritage sites. The visitor rents a cassette player, headphones and a tape in the appropriate language and takes a self-guided tour. The narration provides the visitor with directions and descriptions of selected site elements. For sites associated with historical figures whose voices survive on recordings, it is often effective to incorporate their voice in the narration. The use of a prominent individual's voice to narrate the tour can also add interest to the experience. Such presentations can last from 30 to 60 minutes.

Pre-Recorded Station Stops

Often used in conjunction with a permanently mounted exhibit, prerecorded voice narration is activated by visitors pushing a button. Special attention has to be paid to the audio level of such narration so that it does not disturb other visitors. These presentations are usually brief, lasting no more than one or two minutes.

Car Radio

At large sites, where visitors may have to drive long distances by automobile, low-frequency radio can give directions and narratives. Additionally, radio can be used to guide arriving traffic to unloading points and parking lots.

Sound and Light Shows (Son et Lumiere)

Some World Heritage Sites offer son et lumiere shows to motivate and educate their visitors. Although this dramatic presentation may serve as a significant source of revenue, it can also be the source of many problems.

Entrepreneurs who produce these shows and sell the expensive lighting equipment they require tend to exaggerate potential revenue and dismiss potential problems. The first question to ask is, who will attend the show, day-in, day-out, year-round, year after year? Expensive to install and operate, sound and light shows can seldom survive on local traffic or as mere weekend attractions. Most are scheduled for the height of the tourist season. Tour operators should be consulted as to whether they will include the show in their packages; it is senseless to proceed with this technique if tour operators are uninterested.

Begin with a feasibility study. Beware of figures presented by suppliers or producers. While investment costs can be determined easily, be sure there is careful financial analysis of anticipated revenues. Involve the national tourism office in estimating projected revenues. Seek private advice from tour operators. Contact colleagues in other countries with similar installations to get the benefit of their experience and knowledge.

If the decision is to proceed, reserve contractual rights over final script approval, which must accurately portray the history of the site in a dignified fashion. Avoid overly theatrical scripts.

The system's installation and design must respect the historical fabric of the site and impose only minimal interventions in its appearance. All physical interventions should be reversible. The materials used in the installation should be compatible with the historical and natural colors of the site.

Son et lumiere requires a highly sophisticated electronic system. All installation plans must be approved in advance by the site administrator. The contract must provide for direct day-to-day supervision of the contractor's employees as they set up the show.

The placement and concealment of wiring systems and the enclosure of lighting and sound systems require thorough consideration. It must be remembered that such systems will require sustained, ongoing maintenance and should be accessible for servicing. Every installation decision should be based on how it will affect the day-time visitor's opportunity to photograph the site and enjoy an uncluttered experience.

Many son et lumiere presentations, especially at large sites, require the movement of masses of people through the site in a darkened environment. Adequate safety lighting is essential. Permanent low-level lighting, directed at primary walkways may have to be supplemented by hand-held directional lighting used by the site's guard staff during the performances.

Typically sound and light shows combine sequential mass movements of visitors through the site, followed by a finale before a seated audience. The placement and design of fixed seating can have a major impact on the physical appearance of the cultural site. Seats may be portable chairs, benches or fixed bleachers. It is especially important when using bleachers to be sure that they are sensitively positioned so as not to be visually disruptive. Any fixed seating arrangement should be designed so that it can be easily removed once the son et lumiere program is discontinued.

Guides

The skill and quality of guides can make or break a site's reputation. They need to be carefully selected, trained, monitored, evaluated and motivated. Several site policy issues relate to guides. Will site guides be limited to salaried staff? Will volunteers by recruited and trained? Will outside guides be allowed on the site?

- **Site-Employed Guides:**
  Limiting guides to those on staff will usually provide the best quality control in the selection of candidates, consistency of training, evaluation of presentation and, if necessary, termination. It is often desirable to have staff guides be distinguishable by uniforms--appropriate period-clothing, a distinctive jacket, hat or emblem. It is vitally important to develop and maintain an ongoing training program for all guides, paid or volunteer. New recruits need to be properly trained in what they are expected to impart to the visitors. Existing guides need to be periodically retrained to bring them up-to-date on new information and visitor expectations. Where the site is large, guides should be rotated among stations or routes to avoid their becoming stale and boring. Because of their close contact with visitors, guides are in an excellent position to provide feedback to the site administration on current visitor thinking and reactions. Where a membership program exists for the site, i.e., a national trust or "A Friends of . . ." group, guides can be given incentives to attract new members. If guides are salaried, a policy needs to be formulated with regard to the solicitation and acceptance of tips from visitors. Many sites make use of volunteer guides or docents whose training is handled in the same fashion as that of paid guides. Docents may have the advantage of bringing great enthusiasm and a desire to spread appreciation of the site. The monitoring of site guides is especially important. At random intervals, a qualified consultant or professional colleague, unknown to the guides, should be retained to take a tour among regular visitors and prepare a written evaluation on the quality of the guides' work. These reports should be used in conducting the annual performance evaluation of each guide.
- **Outside Guides:**
  Access by any outside, non-staff guide to the site should be governed by a licensing procedure. Be in a position to exercise quality control over what these guides are presenting to visitors. Depending on the country, these procedures may be the administrative responsibility of the national tourism office or the ministry of culture. Regulations need to be developed and applied concerning use of portable loudspeakers, group tour signs and the sale of any items within the site.

Accommodation of Special Visitors

Certain World Heritage Sites may have to be closed to the general public on days of particular religious or national significance. These closings should be publicized well in advance. On these occasions, visitors with a religious or patriotic affiliation merit special attention. Their appreciation of the site and their ties to it are strong and constant. They also are people who could provide support to the site in many ways. Special interpretive materials produced for their visits might emphasize recent research findings of interest to them or specific site conservation needs that they might be motivated to support.

Special Exhibits for Visually Impaired Visitors

Some sites have instituted special programmed tours for persons with low or no vision, who need more detailed narration to grasp the significance of the site. Small site models that through touching convey the size, scale and organization of the site are popular instructive tools.

Languages

In addition to the national language, it is important to provide basic interpretation in at least the language of the largest number of international visitors. Multilingual versions should be considered for the site brochure, directional signs, site maps, exhibit labels and audio-cassette tours.

Visitor Satisfaction Surveys

To know how effective the staff are in presenting the site to the visiting public, periodically conduct visitor surveys. The survey can be done by interviewing a cross-section of visitors or by giving them a questionnaire, which needs to be kept simple and direct with only the most important questions being asked. To create a long-term database, standardize the questions and don't change them each time a survey is taken. Set up the survey so that the visitor only needs to check boxes or provide a number (1-5) corresponding to strong agreement or disagreement. Seek advice from individuals or firms experienced in conducting and evaluating public-opinion surveys.

Another technique to consider is the "focus group." Here, a small number of visitors are invited to meet with a professional interviewer, to jointly discuss their views and responses to a set of issues and questions. For their participation in such a group exercise, which can give important information, you may wish to present them with a small gift or complimentary meal.

Suomenlinna, Finland: Tags and graffiti are difficult to remove without causing even greater damage to the surface of structures at Suomenlinna Island Fortress in Helsinki, Finland. *Photo by Governing Body of Suomenlinna, R. Amper, courtesy of Heikki Lahdenmaki.*

Suomenlinna, Finland : The historic site of Suomenlinna Island Fortress in Helsinki, Finland, offers both a convenient and aesthetic environment for leisure. *Photo by Governing Body of Suomenlinna, R. Amper, courtesy of Heikki Lahdenmaki.*

Safranbolu, Turkey: A general view of traditional Turkish wooden houses in Safranbolu, Turkey, one of which dating to the 18th century has been converted into a hotel. *Photo by Nur Urfalioglu, Istanbul, Turkey.*

Quito, Ecuador: Balancing the needs of contemporary inhabitants of Quito, Ecuador, with tourists drawn to its colonial center requires involving representatives of the town in conservation efforts. *Photo courtesy of UNESCO.*

Venice, Italy: A 1989 concert by the rock and roll group Pink Floyd in Venice, Italy, threatened its fragile urban environment. *Photo by Mark Smith, courtesy of World Monuments Fund, New York, NY.*

Mesa Verde, Colorado, U.S.A.: The National Park Service has planned for extensive tourism at the fragile archaeological site of Mesa Verde in Colorado. *Photo courtesy of Department of the Interior, Mesa Verde National Park, National Park Service.*

Elephant Caves, India: Before restoration of pillars at Elephanta Caves in India. *Photo courtesy of Vikas Dilawari, Bombay, India.*

Elephant Caves, India: After restoration at Elephanta Caves using controversial technique of reinforced concrete imitating the original stone/rock cut pillars. *Photo courtesy of Vikas Dilawari, Bombay, India.*

Indonesian crafts: Traditional crafts at an Indonesian site maintain heritage fabric by progressive renewal. *Photo by Graham Brooks, Australia.*

Dance at Angkor Wat, Cambodia: Traditional dance performances of the Cambodian Royal Dancers at Angkor Wat and Preah Khan. *Photo by John Stubbs, courtesy of the World Monuments Fund, New York, N.Y.*

Stairs at Olympia, Greece: Protective walkway at Olympia in Greece is a low-key visual intrusion enabling tourists to travel around the site without doing harm. *Photo by Graham Brooks, Australia.*

Caesarea pavement, Israel: An excellent interpretation of an old pavement at Caesarea in Israel extended by matching work. *Photo by Graham Brooks, Australia.*

Multilingual sign, Jerusalem, Israel: Multi-lingual street signage in Jerusalem reinforces historical messages and gives tourists important information. *Photo by Graham Brooks, Australia.*

Pont du Gard, Nimes, France: Buses are allowed to park too close to the Pont du Gard, the historic Roman bridge in southern France. *Photo by Graham Brooks, Australia.*

Angkor, Cambodia: These heads will replace those missing from the bearers lining the eastern gate of the Angkor Thom complex in Cambodia. Pilferers, vandals and art dealers place a high priority on heads, feet, and hands of Khmer sculpture for illicit trade. *Photo by Scott K. Cunliffe, Cultural Management Consultants, Marina del Rey, California.*

Son et lumiere, Old City of Jerusalem, Israel: Son et lumiere in the old city of Jerusalem effectively tells a story going back thousands of years but raises questions about such dramatic spectacles at World Heritage Sites. *Photo by Graham Brooks, Australia.*

World Heritage Convention

Convention Concerning the Protection of the World Cultural and Natural Heritage

Adopted by the General Conference of UNESCO at its seventeenth session, Paris, 16 November 1972.

THE GENERAL CONFERENCE of the United Nations Education, Scientific and Cultural Organization meeting in Paris from 17 October to 21 November 1972, at its seventeenth session,

Noting that the cultural heritage and the natural heritage are increasingly threatened with destruction not only by the traditional causes of decay, but also by changing social and economic conditions which aggravate the situation with even more formidable phenomena of damage or destruction,

Considering that deterioration or disappearance of any item of the cultural or natural heritage constitutes a harmful impoverishment of the heritage of all the nations of the world,

Considering that protection of this heritage at the national level often remains incomplete because of the scale of the resources which it requires and of the insufficient economic, scientific, and technological resources of the country where the property to be protected is situated,

Recalling that the Constitution of the Organization provides that it will maintain, increase, and diffuse knowledge by assuring the conservation and protection of the world's heritage, and recommending to the nations concerned the necessary international conventions,

Considering that the existing international conventions, recommendations and resolutions concerning cultural and natural property demonstrate the importance, for all the peoples of the world, of safeguarding this unique and irreplaceable property, to whatever people it may belong,

Considering that parts of the cultural or natural heritage are of outstanding interest and therefore need to be preserved as part of the world heritage of mankind as a whole,

Considering that in view of the magnitude and gravity of the new dangers threatening them, it is incumbent on the international community as a whole to participate in the protection of the cultural and natural heritage of outstanding universal value, by the granting of collective assistance which, although not taking the place of action by the State concerned, will serve as an efficient complement thereto,

Considering that it is essential for this purpose to adopt new provisions in the form of a convention establishing an effective system of collective protection of the cultural and natural heritage of outstanding universal value, organized on a permanent basis and in accordance with modern sc ientific methods,

Having decided, at its sixteenth session, that this question should be made the subject of an international convention,

Adopts this sixteenth day of November 1972 this Convention.

I. DEFINITION OF THE CULTURAL AND NATURAL HERITAGE

Article 1

For the purpose of this Convention, the following shall be considered as «cultural heritage»:

monuments: architectural works, works of monumental sculpture and painting, elements or structures of an archeological nature, inscriptions, cave dwellings and combinations of features, which are of outstanding universal value from the point of view of history, art or science;

groups of buildings: groups of separate or connected buildings which, because of their architecture, their homogeneity or their place in the landscape, are of outstanding universal value from the point of view of history, art or science;

sites: works of man or the combined works of nature and man, and areas including archaeological sites which are of outstanding universal value from the historical, aesthetic, ethnological or anthropological point of view.

Article 2

For the purposes of this Convention, the following shall be considered as «natural heritage»:

natural features consisting of physical and biological formations or groups of such formations, which are of outstanding universal value from the aesthetic or scientific point of view;

geological and physiographical formations and precisely delineated areas which constitute the habitat of threatened species of animals and plants of outstanding universal value from the point of view of science or conservation;
natural sites or precisely delineated natural areas of

outstanding universal value from the point of view of science, conservation or natural beauty.

Article 3

It is for each State Party to this Convention to identify and delineate the different properties situated on its territory mentioned in Articles 1 and 2 above.

II. NATIONAL PROTECTION AND INTERNATIONAL PROTECTION OF THE CULTURAL AND NATURAL HERITAGE

Article 4

Each State Party to this Convention recognizes that the duty of ensuring the identification, protection, conservation, presentation and transmission to future generations of the cultural and natural heritage referred to in Articles 1 and 2 and situated on its territory, belongs primarily to that State. It will do all it can to this end, to the utmost of its own resources and, where appropriate, with any international assistance and co-operation, in particular, financial, artistic, scientific and technical, which it may be able to obtain.

Article 5

To ensure that effective and active measures are taken for the protection, conservation and presentation of the cultural and natural heritage situated on its territory, each State Party to this Convention shall endeavor, in so far as possible, and as appropriate for each country:

a. to adopt a general policy which aims to give the cultural and natural heritage a function in the life of the community and to integrate the protection of that heritage into comprehensive planning programmes;

b. to set up within its territories, where such services do not exist, one or more services for the protection, conservation and presentation of the cultural and natural heritage with an appropriate staff and possessing the means to discharge their functions;

c. to develop scientific and technical studies and research and to work out such operating methods as will make the State capable of counteracting the dangers that threaten its cultural or natural heritage;

d. to take the appropriate legal, scientific, technical, administrative and financial measures necessary for the identification, protection, conservation, presentation and rehabilitation of this heritage; and

e. to foster the establishment or development of national or regional centres for training in the protection, conservation and presentation of the cultural and natural heritage and to encourage scientific research in this field.

Article 6

1. Whilst fully respecting the sovereignty of the States on whose territory the cultural and natural heritage mentioned in Articles 1 and 2 is situated, and without prejudice to property right provided by national legislation, the States Parties to this Convention recognize that such heritage constitutes a world heritage for whose protection it is the duty of the international community as a whole to co-operate.

2. The States Parties undertake, in accordance with the provisions of this Convention, to give their help in the identification, protection, conservation and presentation of the cultural and natural heritage referred to in paragraphs 2 and 4 of Article 11 if the States on whose territory it is situated so request.

3. Each State Party to this Convention undertakes not to take any deliberate measures which might damage directly or indirectly the cultural and natural heritage referred to in Articles 1 and 2 situated on the territory of other States Parties to this Convention.

Article 7

For the purpose of this Convention, international protection of the world cultural and natural heritage shall be understood to mean the establishment of a system of international co-operation and assistance designed to support States Parties to the Convention in their efforts to conserve and identify that heritage.

III. INTERGOVERNMENTAL COMMITTEE FOR THE PROTECTION OF THE WORLD CULTURAL AND NATURAL HERITAGE

Article 8

1. An Intergovernmental Committee for the Protection of the Cultural and Natural Heritage of Outstanding Universal Value, called «the World Heritage Committee», is hereby established within the United Nations Education, Scientific and Cultural Organization. It shall be composed of 15 States Parties to the Convention, elected by States Parties to the Convention meeting in general assembly during the ordinary session of the General Conference of the United Nations Educational, Scientific and Cultural Organization. The number of States members of the Committee shall be increased

to 21 as from the date of the ordinary session of the General Conference following the entry into force of this Convention for at least 40 States.

2. Election of members of the Committee shall ensure an equitable representation of the different regions and cultures of the world.

3. A representative of the International Centre for the Study of the Preservation and Restoration of Cultural Property (Rome Centre), a representative of the International Council of Monuments and Sites (ICOMOS) and a representative of the International Union for Conservation of Nature and Natural Resources (IUCN), to whom may be added, at the request of States Parties to the Convention meeting in general assembly during the ordinary sessions of the General Conference of the United Nations Educational, Scientific and Cultural Organization, representatives of other intergovernmental or non-governmental organizations, with similar objectives, may attend the meetings of the Committee in an advisory capacity.

Article 9

1. The term of office of States members of the World Heritage Committee shall extend from the end of the ordinary session of the General Conference during which they are elected until the end of its third subsequent ordinary session.

2. The term of office of one-third of the members designated at the time of the first election shall, however, cease at the end of the first ordinary session of the General Conference following that at which they were elected; and the term of office of a further third of the members designated at the same time shall cease at the end of the second ordinary session of the General Conference following that at which they were elected. The names of these members shall be chosen by lot by the President of the General Conference of the United Nations Education, Scientific and Cultural Organization after the first election.

3. States members of the Committee shall choose as their representatives persons qualified in the field of the cultural or natural heritage.

Article 10

1. The World Heritage Committee shall adopt its Rules of Procedure.

2. The Committee may at any time invite public or private organizations or individuals to participate in its meetings for consultation on particular problems.

3. The Committee may create such consultative bodies as it deems necessary for the performance of its functions.

Article 11

1. Every State Party to this Convention shall, in so far as possible, submit to the World Heritage Committee an inventory of property forming part of the cultural and natural heritage, situated in its territory and suitable for inclusion in the list provided for in paragraph 2 of this Article. This inventory, which shall not be considered exhaustive, shall include documentation about the location of the property in question and its significance.

2. On the basis of the inventories submitted by States in accordance with paragraph 1, the Committee shall establish, keep up to date and publish, under the title of «World Heritage List,» a list of properties forming part of the cultural heritage and natural heritage, as defined in Articles 1 and 2 of this Convention, which it considers as having outstanding universal value in terms of such criteria as it shall have established. An updated list shall be distributed at least every two years.

3. The inclusion of a property in the World Heritage List requires the consent of the State concerned. The inclusion of a property situated in a territory, sovereignty or jurisdiction over which is claimed by more than one State shall in no way prejudice the rights of the parties to the dispute.

4. The Committee shall establish, keep up to date and publish, whenever circumstances shall so require, under the title of «list of World Heritage in Danger», a list of the property appearing in the World Heritage List for the conservation of which major operations are necessary and for which assistance has been requested under this Convention. This list shall contain an estimate of the cost of such operations. The list may include only such property forming part of the cultural and natural heritage as is threatened by serious and specific dangers, such as the threat of disappearance caused by accelerated deterioration, large-scale public or private projects or rapid urban or tourist development projects; destruction caused by changes in the use or ownership of the land; major alterations due to unknown causes; abandonment for any reason whatsoever; the outbreak or the threat of an armed conflict; calamities and cataclysms; serious fires, earthquakes, landslides; volcanic eruptions; changes in water level, floods and tidal waves. The Committee may at any time, in case of urgent need, make a new entry in the List of World Heritage in Danger and publicize such entry immediately.

5. The Committee shall define the criteria on the basis of which a property belonging to the cultural or natural heritage may be included in either of the lists mentioned in paragraphs 2 and 4 of this article.

6. Before refusing a request for inclusion in one of the two lists mentioned in paragraphs 2 and 4 of this article, the Committee shall consult the State Party in whose territory the cultural or natural property in question is situated.

7. The Committee shall, with the agreement of the States concerned, co- ordinate and encourage the studies and research needed for the drawing up of the lists referred to in paragraphs 2 and 4 of this article.

Article 12

The fact that a property belonging to the cultural or natural heritage has not been included in either of the two lists mentioned in paragraphs 2 and 4 of Article 11 shall in no way be construed to mean that it does not have an outstanding universal value for purposes other than those resulting from inclusion in these lists.

Article 13

1. The World Heritage Committee shall receive and study requests for international assistance formulated by States Parties to this Convention with respect to property forming part of the cultural or natural heritage, situated in their territories, and included or potentially suitable for inclusion in the lists mentioned referred to in paragraphs 2 and 4 of Article 11. The purpose of such requests may be to secure the protection, conservation, presentation or rehabilitation of such property.

2. Requests for international assistance under paragraph 1 of this article may also be concerned with identification of cultural or natural property defined in Articles 1 and 2, when preliminary investigations have shown that further inquiries would be justified.

3. The Committee shall decide on the action to be taken with regard to these requests, determine where appropriate, the nature and extent of its assistance, and authorize the conclusion, on its behalf, of the necessary arrangements with the government concerned.

4. The Committee shall determine an order of priorities for its operations. It shall in so doing bear in mind the respective importance for the world cultural and natural heritage of the property requiring protection, the need to give international assistance to the property most representative

of a natural environment or of the genius and the history of the peoples of the world, the urgency of the work to be done, the resources available to the States on whose territory the threatened property is situated and in particular the extent to which they are able to safeguard such property by their own means.

5. The Committee shall draw up, keep up to date and publicize a list of property for which international assistance has been granted.

6. The Committee shall decide on the use of the resources of the Fund established under Article 15 of this Convention. It shall seek ways of increasing these resources and shall take all useful steps to this end.

7. The Committee shall co-operate with international and national governmental and non-governmental organizations having objectives similar to those of this Convention. For the implementation of its programmes and projects, the Committee may call on such organizations, particularly the International Centre for the Study of the Preservation and Restoration of cultural Property (the Rome Centre), the International Council of Monuments and Sites (ICOMOS) and the International Union for Conservation of Nature and Natural Resources (IUCN), as well as on public and private bodies and individuals.

8. Decisions of the Committee shall be taken by a majority of two-thirds of its members present and voting. A majority of the members of the Committee shall constitute a quorum.

Article 14

1. The World Heritage Committee shall be assisted by a Secretariat appointed by the Director-General of the United Nations Educational, Scientific and Cultural Organization.

2. The Director-General of the United Nations Educational, Scientific and Cultural Organization, utilizing to the fullest extent possible the services of the International Centre for the Study of the Preservation and the Restoration of Cultural Property (the Rome Centre), the International Council of Monuments and Sites (ICOMOS) and the International Union for Conservation of Nature and Natural Resources (IUCN) in their respective areas of competence and capability, shall prepare the Committee's documentation and the agenda of its meetings and shall have the responsibility for the implementation of its decisions.

IV. FUND FOR THE PROTECTION OF THE WORLD CULTURAL AND NATURAL HERITAGE

Article 15

1. A Fund for the Protection of the World Cultural and Natural Heritage of Outstanding Universal Value, called «the World Heritage Fund», is hereby established.

2. The Fund shall constitute a trust fund, in conformity with the provisions of the Financial Regulations of the United Nations Educational, Scientific and Cultural Organization.

3. The resources of the Fund shall consist of:

   a. compulsory and voluntary contributions made by States Parties to this Convention,
   b. Contributions, gifts or bequests which may be made by:
      i. other States;
      ii. the United Nations Educational, Scientific and Cultural Organization, other organizations of the United Nations system, particularly the United Nations Development Programme or other intergovernmental organizations;
      iii. public or private bodies or individuals;

   c. any interest due on the resources of the Fund;
   d. funds raised by collections and receipts from events organized for the benefit of the fund; and
   e. all other resources authorized by the Fund's regulations, as drawn up by the World Heritage Committee.

4. Contributions to the Fund and other forms of assistance made available to the Committee may be used only for such purposes as the Committee shall define. The Committee may accept contributions to be used only for a certain programme or project, provided that the Committee shall have decided on the implementation of such programme or project. No political conditions may be attached to contributions made to the Fund.

Article 16

1. Without prejudice to any supplementary voluntary contribution, the States Parties to this Convention undertake to pay regularly, every two years, to the World Heritage Fund, contributions, the amount of which, in the form of a uniform percentage applicable to all States, shall be determined by the General Assembly of States Parties to the Convention, meeting during the sessions of the General Conference of the United Nations Educational, Scientific and Cultural Organization. This decision of the General Assembly

requires the majority of the States Parties present and voting, which have not made the declaration referred to in paragraph 2 of this Article. In no case shall the compulsory contribution of States Parties to the Convention exceed 1% of the contribution to the regular budget of the United Nations Educational, Scientific and Cultural Organization.

2. However, each State referred to in Article 31 or in Article 32 of this Convention may declare, at the time of the deposit of its instrument of ratification, acceptance or accession, that it shall not be bound by the provisions of paragraph 1 of this Article.

3. A State Party to the Convention which has made the declaration referred to in paragraph 2 of this Article may at any time withdraw the said declaration by notifying the Director-General of the United Nations Educational, Scientific and Cultural Organization. However, the withdrawal of the declaration shall not take effect in regard to the compulsory contribution due by the State until the date of the subsequent General Assembly of States parties to the Convention.

4. In order that the Committee may be able to plan its operations effectively, the contributions of States Parties to this Convention which have made the declaration referred to in paragraph 2 of this Article, shall be paid on a regular basis, at least every two years, and should not be less than the contributions which they should have paid if they had been bound by the provisions of paragraph 1 of this Article.

5. Any State Party to the Convention which is in arrears with the payment of its compulsory or voluntary contribution for the current year and the calendar year immediately preceding it shall not be eligible as a Member of the World Heritage Committee, although this provision shall not apply to the first election.

The terms of office of any such State which is already a member of the Committee shall terminate at the time of the elections provided for in Article 8, paragraph 1 of this Convention.

Article 17

The States Parties to this Convention shall consider or encourage the establishment of national public and private foundations or associations whose purpose is to invite donations for the protection of the cultural and natural heritage as defined in Articles 1 and 2 of this Convention.

Article 18

The States Parties to this Convention shall give their assistance to international fund-raising campaigns organized for the World Heritage Fund under the auspices of the United Nations Educational, Scientific and Cultural Organization. They shall facilitate collections made by the bodies mentioned in paragraph 3 of Article 15 for this purpose.

V. CONDITIONS AND ARRANGEMENTS FOR INTERNATIONAL ASSISTANCE

Article 19

Any State Party to this Convention may request international assistance for property forming part of the cultural or natural heritage of outstanding universal value situated within its territory. It shall submit with its request such information and documentation provided for in Article 21 as it has in its possession and as will enable the Committee to come to a decision.

Article 20

Subject to the provisions of paragraph 2 of Article 13, sub-paragraph (c) of Article 22 and Article 23, international assistance provided for by this Convention may be granted only to property forming part of the cultural and natural heritage which the World Heritage Committee has decided, or may decide, to enter in one of the lists mentioned in paragraphs 2 and 4 of Article 11.

Article 21

1. The World Heritage Committee shall define the procedure by which requests to it for international assistance shall be considered and shall specify the content of the request, which should define the operation contemplated, the work that is necessary, the expected cost thereof, the degree of urgency and the reasons why the resources of the State requesting assistance do not allow it to meet all the expenses. Such requests must be supported by experts' reports whenever possible.

2. Requests based upon disasters or natural calamities should, by reasons of the urgent work which they may involve, be given immediate, priority consideration by the Committee, which should have a reserve fund at its disposal against such contingencies.

3. Before coming to a decision, the Committee shall carry out such studies and consultations as it deems necessary.

Article 22

Assistance granted by the World Heritage Fund may take the following forms:

a. studies concerning the artistic, scientific and technical problems raised by the protection, conservation, presentation and rehabilitation of the cultural and natural heritage, as defined in paragraphs 2 and 4 of Article 11 of this Convention;

b. provisions of experts, technicians and skilled labour to ensure that the approved work is correctly carried out;

c. training of staff and specialists at all levels in the field of identification, protection, conservation, presentation and rehabilitation of the cultural and natural heritage;

d. supply of equipment which the State concerned does not possess or is not in a position to acquire;

e. low-interest or interest-free loans which might be repayable on a long-term basis;

f. the granting, in exceptional cases and for special reasons, of non-repayable subsidies.

Article 23

The World Heritage Committee may also provide international assistance to national or regional centres for the training of staff and specialists at all levels in the field of identification, protection, conservation, presentation and rehabilitation of the cultural and natural heritage.

Article 24

International assistance on a large scale shall be preceded by detailed scientific, economic and technical studies. These studies shall draw upon the most advanced techniques for the protection, conservation, presentation and rehabilitation of the natural and cultural heritage and shall be consistent with the objectives of this Convention. The studies shall also seek means of making rational use of the resources available in the State concerned.

Article 25

As a general rule, only part of the cost of work necessary shall be borne by the international community. The contribution of the State benefiting from international assistance shall constitute a substantial share of the resources devoted to each programme or project, unless its resources do not permit this.

Article 26

The World Heritage Committee and the recipient State shall define in the agreement they conclude the conditions in which a programme or project for which international assistance under the terms of this Convention is provided, shall be carried out. It shall be the responsibility of the State receiving such international assistance to continue to protect, conserve and present the property so safeguarded, in observance of the conditions laid down by the agreement.

VI. EDUCATIONAL PROGRAMMES

Article 27

1. The States Parties to this Convention shall endeavor by all appropriate means, and in particular by educational and information programmes, to strengthen appreciation and respect by their peoples of the cultural and natural heritage defined in Articles 1 and 2 of the Convention.

2. They shall undertake to keep the public broadly informed of the dangers threatening this heritage and of the activities carried on in pursuance of this Convention.

Article 28

States Parties to this Convention which receive international assistance under the Convention shall take appropriate measures to make known the importance of the property for which assistance has been received and the role played by such assistance.

VII. REPORTS

Article 29

1. The States Parties to this Convention shall, in the reports which they submit to the General Conference of the United Nations Educational, Scientific and Cultural Organization on dates and in a manner to be determined by it, give information on the legislative and administrative provisions which they have adopted and other action which they have taken for the application of this Convention, together with details of the experience acquired in this field.

2. These reports shall be brought to the attention of the World Heritage Committee.

3. The Committee shall submit a report on its activities at each of the ordinary sessions of the General Conference of the United Nations Educational, Scientific and Cultural Organization.

VIII. FINAL CLAUSES

Article 30

This Convention is drawn up in Arabic, English, French, Russian and Spanish, the five texts being equally authoritative.

Article 31

1. This Convention shall be subject to ratification or acceptance by States members of the United Nations Educational, Scientific and Cultural Organization in accordance with their respective constitutional procedures.

2. The instruments of ratification or acceptance shall be deposited with the Director-General of the United Nations Educational, Scientific and Cultural Organization.

Article 32

1. This Convention shall be open to accession by all States not members of the United Nations Educational, Scientific and Cultural Organization which are invited by the General Conference of the Organization to accede to it.

2. Accession shall be effected by the deposit of an instrument of accession with the Director-General of the United Nations Educational, Scientific and Cultural Organization.

Article 33

This Convention shall enter into force three months after the date of the deposit of the twentieth instrument of ratification, acceptance or accession, but only with respect to those States which have deposited their respective instruments of ratification, acceptance or accession on or before that date. It shall enter into force with respect to any other State three months after the deposit of its instrument of ratification, acceptance or accession.

Article 34

The following provisions shall apply to those States Parties to this Convention which have a federal or non-unitary constitutional system:

a. with regard to the provisions of this Convention, the implementation of which comes under the legal jurisdiction of the federal or central legislative power, the obligations of the federal or central government shall be the same as for those States parties which are not federal States;

b. with regard to the provisions of this Convention, the implementation of which comes under the legal jurisdiction of individual constituent States, countries, provinces or cantons that are not obliged by the constitutional system of the federation to take legislative measures, the federal government shall inform the competent authorities of such States, countries, provinces or cantons of the said provisions, with its recommendation for their adoption.

Article 35

1. Each State Party to this Convention may denounce the Convention.

2. The denunciation shall be notified by an instrument in writing, deposited with the Director-General of the United Nations Educational, Scientific and Cultural Organization.

3. The denunciation shall take effect twelve months after the receipt of the instrument of denunciation. It shall not affect the financial obligations of the denouncing State until the date on which the withdrawal takes effect.

Article 36

The Director-General of the United Nations Educational, Scientific and Cultural Organization shall inform the States members of the Organization, the States not members of the Organization which are referred to in Article 32, as well as the United Nations, of the deposit of all the instruments of ratification, acceptance, or accession provided for in Articles 31 and 32, and of the denunciations provided for in Article 35.

Article 37

1. This Convention may be revised by the General Conference of the United Nations Educational, Scientific and Cultural Organization. Any such revision shall, however, bind only the States which shall become Parties to the revising convention.

2. If the General Conference should adopt a new convention revising this Convention in whole or in part, then, unless the new convention otherwise provides, this Convention shall cease to be open to ratification, acceptance or accession, as from the date on which the new revising convention enters into force.

Article 38

In conformity with Article 102 of the Charter of the United Nations, this Convention shall be registered with the Secretariat of the United Nations at the request of the Director-General of the United Nations Educational, Scientific and Cultural Organization.

Done in Paris, this twenty-third day of November 1972, in two authentic copies bearing the signature of the President of the seventeenth session of the General Conference and of the Director-General of the United Nations Educational, Scientific and Cultural Organization, which shall be deposited in the archives of the United Nations Educational, Scientific and Cultural Organization, and certified true copies of which shall be delivered to all the States referred to in Articles 31 and 32 as well as to the United Nations.

World Heritage Definitions and Criteria

Since the ratification of the World Heritage Convention, the World Heritage Committee has developed operational guidelines which it maintains and revises as necessary. These operational guidelines constitute what amounts to a substantial technical operating manual. For more information or a copy of the manual, write to the World Heritage Center, 7 Place de Fontenoy, 75352 Paris 07 SP, France (E-mail: wh-info@unesco.org; Website: www.http://www.unesco.org/whc). Below are excerpted sections from the operational guidelines most useful for reference in the context of this volume. This chapter begins with three definitions taken from the World Heritage Convention.

World Heritage Definitions

The following definitions are set out in Article 1 of the World Heritage Convention.

- **Monuments:**
  architectural works, works of monumental sculpture and painting, elements or structures of an archeological nature, inscriptions, cave dwellings and combinations of features, which are of outstanding universal value from the point of view of history, art or science;
- **Groups of Buildings:**
  groups of separate or connected buildings which, because of their architecture, their homogeneity or their place in the landscape, are of outstanding universal value from the point of view of history, art or science;
- **Sites:**
  works of man or the combined works of nature and of man, and areas including archeological sites which are of outstanding universal value from the historical, aesthetic, ethnological or anthropological points of view.

Criteria from the Operational Guidelines

Outstanding Universal Value

(24) A monument, group of buildings or sites - as defined above - which is nominated for inclusion in the World Heritage List will be considered to be of outstanding universal value for the purposes of the Convention when the Committee finds that it meets one or more of the following criteria and the text of authenticity. Each property nominated should therefore:

- represent a masterpiece of human creative genius; or
- exhibit an important interchange of human values, over a span of time or within a cultural area of the world, on developments in architecture, monumental arts or town-planning and landscaping; or
- bear a unique or at least exceptional testimony to a civilization which has disappeared; or
- be an outstanding example of a type of buildings or architectural ensemble or landscape which illustrates a significant state in history; or
- be an outstanding example of a traditional human settlement or land-use which is representative of a culture especially when it has become vulnerable under the impact of irreversible change; or
- be directly or tangibly associated with events or living traditions, with ideas, or with beliefs, with artistic or literary works of outstanding universal significance (the Committee considers that this criterion should justify inclusion in the List only in exceptional circumstances or in conjunction with other criteria cultural or natural); and

- meet the test of authenticity in design, material, workmanship or setting and in the case of cultural landscapes their distinctive character and components (the Committee stressed that reconstruction is only acceptable if it is carried out on the basis of complete and detailed documentation on the original and to no extent on conjecture).

Criteria for Urban Buildings

(27) Groups of urban buildings eligible for inclusion in the World Heritage List fall into three main categories, namely:

- towns which are no longer inhabited but which provide unchanged archeological evidence of the past; these generally satisfy the criterion of authenticity and their state of conservation can be relatively easily controlled;
- historic towns which are still inhabited and which, by their very nature, have developed and will continue to develop under the influence of socio-economic and cultural change, a situation that renders the assessment of their authenticity more difficult and any conservation policy more problematical;
- new towns of the twentieth century which paradoxically have something in common with both the aforementioned categories: while their original urban organization is clearly recognizable and their authenticity in undeniable, their future is unclear because their development is largely uncontrollable.

(28) The evaluation of towns that are no longer inhabited does not raise any special difficulties other than those related to archeological sites in general: the criteria which call for uniqueness or exemplary character have led to the choice of groups of buildings noteworthy for their purity of style, for the concentrations of monuments they contain and sometimes for their important historical associations. It is important for urban archeological sites to be listed as integral units. A cluster of monuments or a small group of buildings is not adequate to suggest the multiple and complex functions of a city which has disappeared; remains of such a city should be preserved in their entirety together with their natural surroundings whenever possible.

(29) In the case of inhabited historic towns the difficulties are numerous, largely owing to the fragility of their urban fabric (which has in many cases been seriously disrupted since the advent of the industrial era) and the runaway speed with which their surroundings have been urbanized. To qualify for inclusion, towns should compel recognition because of their architectural interest and should not be considered only on the intellectual grounds of the role they may have played in the past, of their value as historical symbols under criterion (vi) for the inclusion of cultural properties in the World Heritage List (see paragraph 24 above). To be eligible for inclusion in the List, the spatial organization, structure, materials, forms and, where possible, functions of a group of buildings should essentially reflect the civilization or succession of civilizations which have prompted the nomination of the property. Four categories can be distinguished:

- Towns which are typical of a specific period of culture, which have been almost wholly preserved and which have remained largely unaffected by subsequent developments. Here the property to be listed is the entire town together with its surroundings, which must also be protected;Towns that have evolved along characteristic lines and have preserved, sometimes in the midst of exceptional natural surroundings, spatial arrangements and structures that are typical of the successive stages in their history. Here the clearly defined historic past takes precedence over the contemporary environment;
- Historic centres that cover exactly the same area as ancient towns and are now enclosed with modern cities. Here it is necessary to determine the precise limits of the property in its widest historical dimensions and to make appropriate provisions for its immediate surroundings;

- Sectors, areas or isolated units which, even in the residual state in which they have survived, provide coherent evidence of the character of a historic town which has disappeared. In such cases surviving areas and buildings should bear sufficient testimony to the former whole.

(30) Historic centres and historic areas should be listed only where they contain a large number of ancient buildings of monumental importance which provide a direct indication of the characteristic features of a town of exceptional interest. Nominations of several isolated and unrelated buildings which allegedly represent, in themselves, a town whose urban fabric has ceased to be discernible, should not be encouraged.

(31) However, nominations could be made regarding properties that occupy a limited space but have had a major influence on the history of town planning. In such cases, the nomination should make it clear that it is the monumental group that is to be listed and that the town is mentioned only incidentally as the place where the property is located. Similarly, if a building of clearly universal significance is located in severely degraded or insufficiently representative urban surroundings, it should, of course, be listed without a special reference to the town.

(32) It is difficult to assess the quality of new towns of the twentieth century. History alone will tell which of them will best serve as examples of contemporary town planning. The examination of the files on these town should be deferred, save under exceptional circumstances.

(33) Under present conditions, preference should be given to the inclusion in the World Heritage List of small or medium-sized urban areas which are in a position to manage any potential growth rather than the great metropolises, on which sufficiently complete information and documentation cannot be provided that would serve as a satisfactory basis for their inclusion in their entirety. In view of the effects which the entry of a town in the World Heritage List could have on its future, such entries should be exceptional. Inclusion in the List implies that legislative and administrative measures have already been taken to ensure the protection of the group of buildings and its environment. Informed awareness on the part of the population concerned, without whose active participation any conservation scheme would be impractical, is also essential.

Maps of Cultural and Cultural/Natural Sites on the World Heritage List

The World Heritage Committee has approved the following cultural properties for inscription on the World Heritage List, under the Convention concerning the Protection of the World Cultural and Natural Heritage (1972). The properties are arranged by continent, in alphabetical order by country and in order of inscription.

(c) **Cultural Site**
(n/c) **Natural and Cultural Site**

Eastern Asia

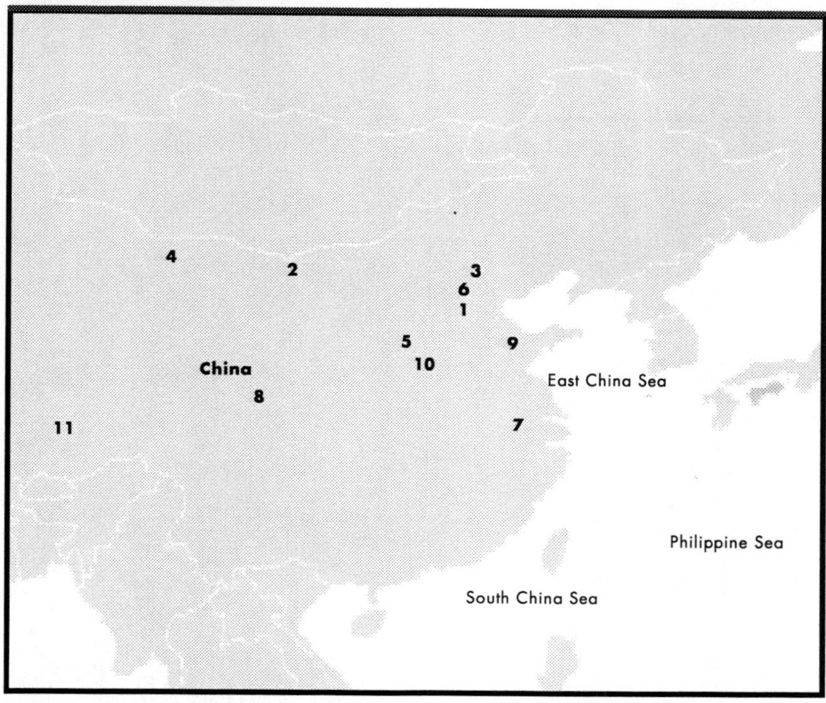

China, People's Republic of

1(n/c) Mount Taishan
2(c) The Great Wall
3(c) Imperial Palace of the Ming and Qing Dynasties
4(c) Mogao Caves
5(c) The Mausoleum of the First Qin Emperor
6(c) Peking Man Site at Zhoukoudian
7(n/c) Mount Huangshan
8(c) The Mountain Resort and Outlying Temples, Chengde
9(c) Temple of Confucius, Cemetery of Confucius, and Kong Family Mansion in Qufu
10(c) Ancient Building Complex in the Wudang Mountains
11(c) The Potala Palace, Lhasa

Southeastern Asia

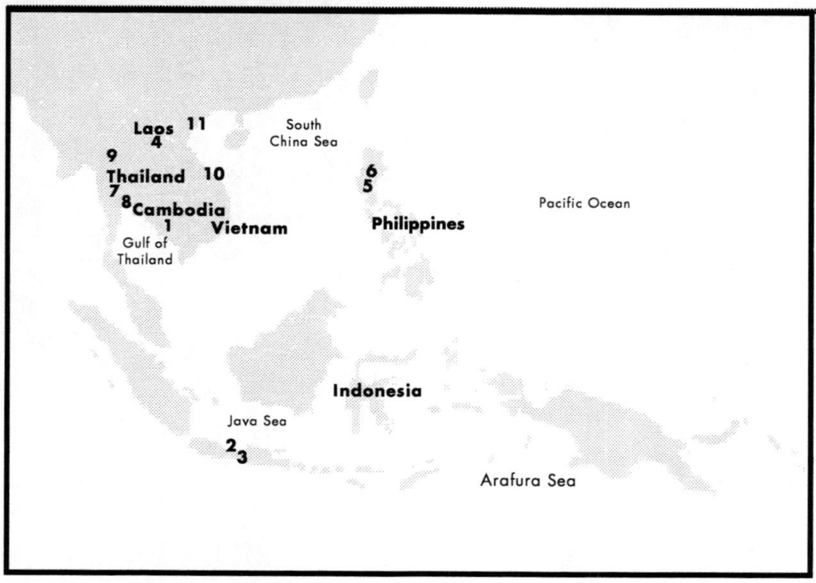

Cambodia
1(c) Angkor

Indonesia
2(c) Borobudur Temple Compound
3(c) Prambanan Temple Compound

Lao People's Democratic Republic
4(c) Town of Luang Prabang

Philippines
5(c) Baroque Churches of the Philippines
6(c) Rice Terrasses of the Philippines Cordilleras

Thailand
7(c) Historic Town of Sukhothai and Associated Historic Towns
8(c) Historic City of Ayutthaya and Associated Historic Towns
9(c) Ban Chiang Archaeological Site

Vietnam
10(c) Hue (Complex of Monuments)
11(c) Ha Long Bay

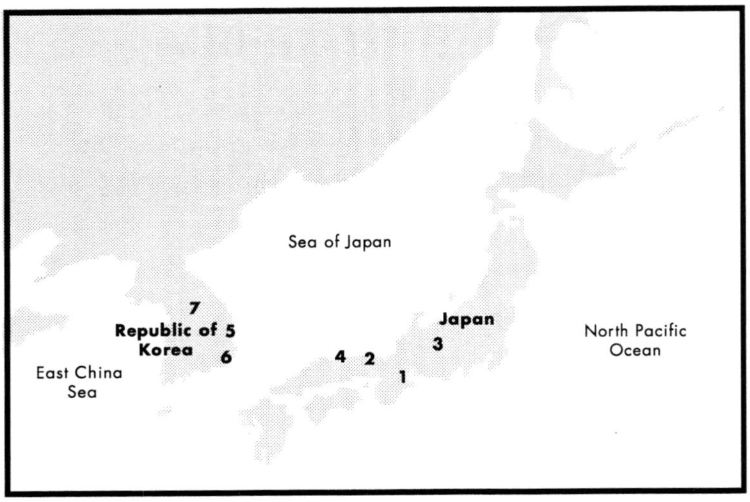

Northern Pacific

Japan
1(c) Himeji-jo
2(c) Buddhist Monuments in the Horyuji Area
3(c) Historic Monuments of Ancient Kyoto (Kyoto, Uji and Otsu Cities)
4(c) Historic Villages of Shirakawa-go and Gokayama

Republic of Korea
5(c) Sokkuram Grotto
6(c) Haiensa Temple Changgyong P'ango, The Depositories for the Tripitaka Koreana Woodblocks
7(c) The Chongmyo Shrine

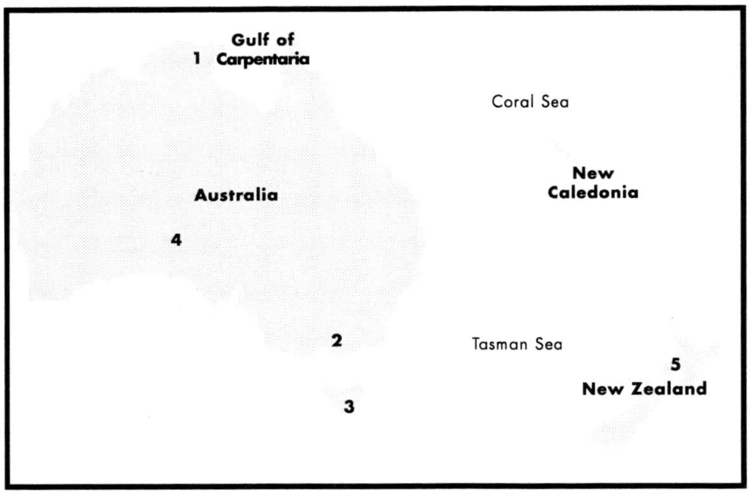

Southern Pacific

Australia
1(n/c) Kakadu National Park
2(n/c) Willandra Lakes Region
3(n/c) Tasmania Wilderness National Parks
4(n/c) Uluru National Park

New Zealand
5(n/c) Tongariro National Park

Central Asia

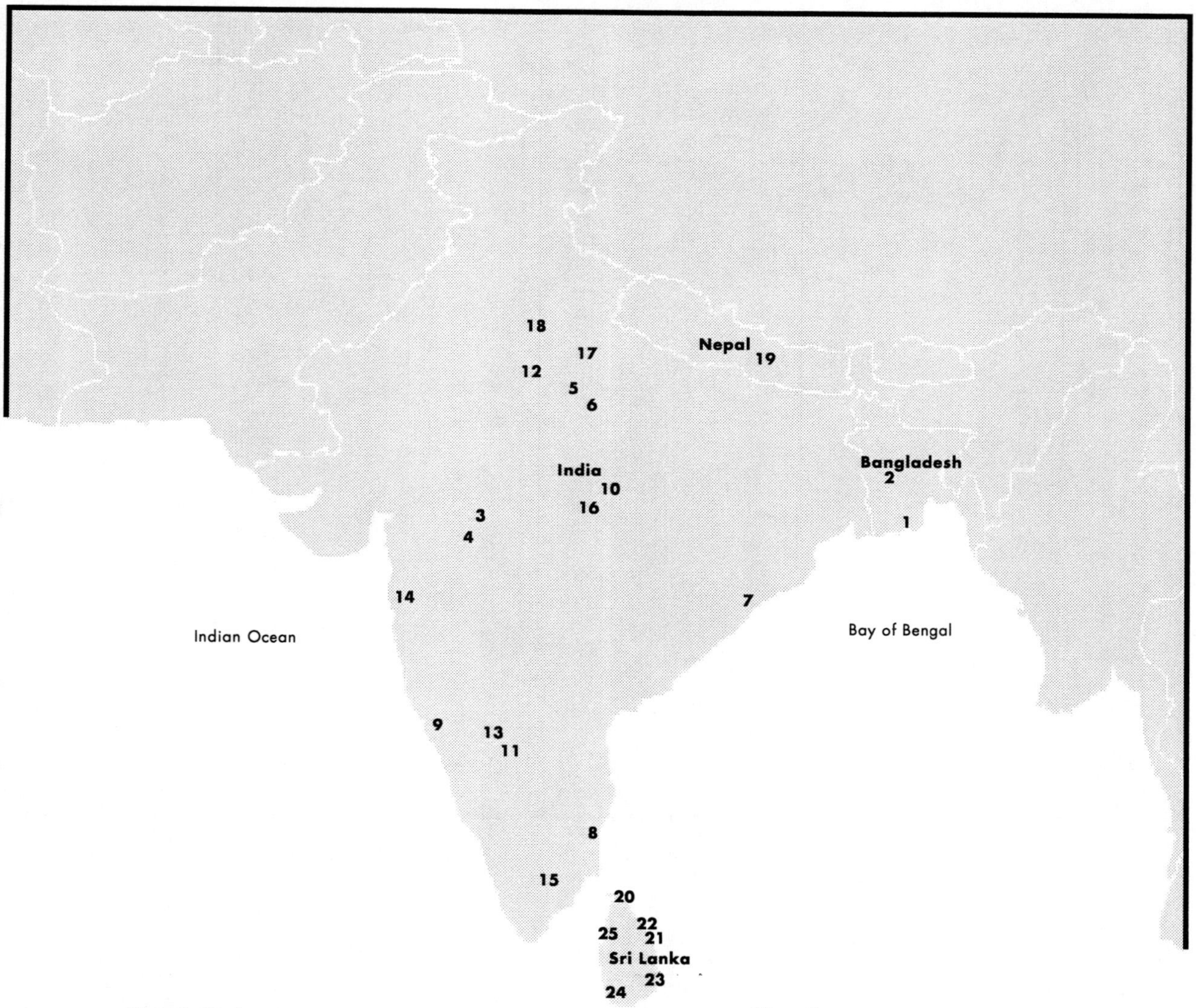

Bangladesh

- 1(c) Historic Mosque City of Bagerhat
- 2(c) Ruins of the Buddhist Vihara at Paharpur

India

- 3(c) Ajanta Caves
- 4(c) Ellora Caves
- 5(c) Agra Fort
- 6(c) Taj Mahal
- 7(c) Sun Temple, Konarak
- 8(c) Group of Monuments at Mahabalipuram
- 9(c) Churches and Convents of Goa
- 10(c) Group of Monuments at Khajuraho
- 11(c) Group of Monuments at Hampi
- 12(c) Fatehpur Sikri
- 13(c) Group of Monuments at Pattadakal
- 14(c) Elephanta Caves
- 15(c) Brihadisvara Temple, Thanjavur
- 16(c) Buddhist Monuments at Sanchi
- 17(c) Humayun's Tomb
- 18(c) Qutb Minar and Its Monuments, Delhi

Nepal

- 19(c) Kathmandu Valley

Sri Lanka

- 20(c) Sacred City of Anuradhapura
- 21(c) Ancient City of Polonnaruwa
- 22(c) Ancient City Sigiriya
- 23(c) Sacred City of Kandy
- 24(c) Old Town of Galle and Its fortifications
- 25(c) Golden Temple of Dambulla

Western and Northern Asia

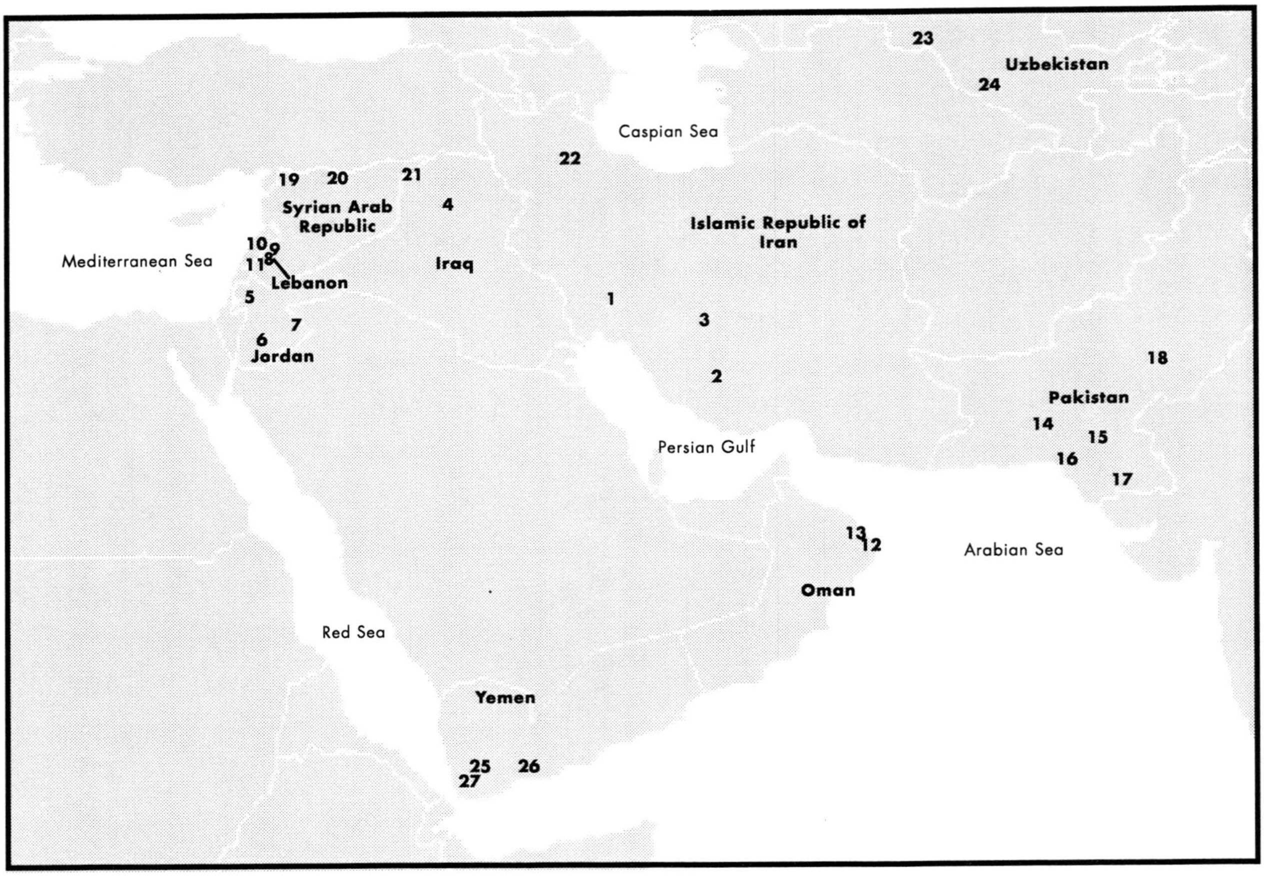

Iran, Islamic Republic of
- 1(c) Tchogha Zanbil
- 2(c) Persepolis
- 3(c) Meidan Emam, Esfahan

Iraq
- 4(c) Hatra

Jordan
- 5(c) Old City of Jerusalem and Its Walls
- 6(c) Petra
- 7(c) Quseir Amra

Lebanon
- 8(c) Anjar
- 9(c) Baalbek
- 10(c) Byblos
- 11(c) Tyr

Oman
- 12(c) Bahla Fort
- 13(c) Archaeological Sites of Bat, Al-Khutm and Al-Ayn

Pakistan
- 14(c) Archaeological Ruins at Moenjodaro
- 15(c) Taxila
- 16(c) Buddhist Ruins of Takht-i-Bahi and Neighboring City Remains at Sahr-i-Bahlol
- 17(c) Historical Monuments of Thatta
- 18(c) Fort and Shalimar Gardens in Lahore

Syrian Arab Republic
- 19(c) Ancient City of Damascus
- 20(c) Ancient City of Bosra
- 21(c) Site of Palmyra
- 22(c) Ancient City of Aleppo

Uzbekistan
- 23(c) Itchan Kala
- 24(c) Historic Center of Boukhara

Yemen Republic
- 25(c) Old City of Sana'a
- 26(c) Old City of Shibam and Its Walls
- 27(c) Historic Town of Zabid

Africa

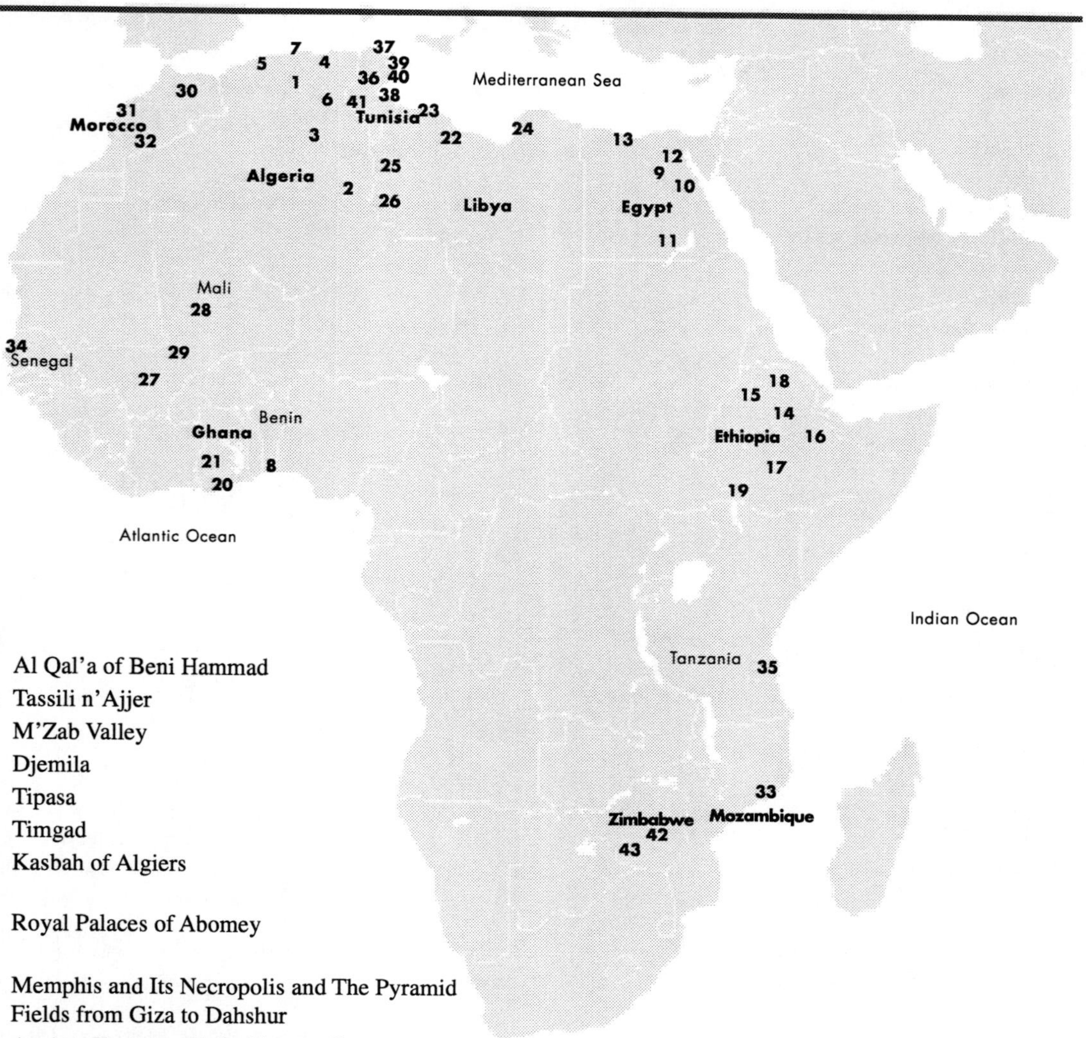

Algeria
- 1(c) Al Qal'a of Beni Hammad
- 2(n/c) Tassili n'Ajjer
- 3(c) M'Zab Valley
- 4(c) Djemila
- 5(c) Tipasa
- 6(c) Timgad
- 7(c) Kasbah of Algiers

Benin
- 8(c) Royal Palaces of Abomey

Egypt
- 9(c) Memphis and Its Necropolis and The Pyramid Fields from Giza to Dahshur
- 10(c) Ancient Thebes with Its Necropolis
- 11(c) Nubian Monuments from Abu Simbel to Philae
- 12(c) Islamic Cairo
- 13(c) Abu Mena

Ethiopia
- 14(c) Rock-hewn Churches of Lalibela
- 15(c) Fasil Ghebbi, Gondar Region
- 16(c) Lower Valley of the Awash
- 17(c) Tiya
- 18(c) Aksum
- 19(c) Lower Valley of the Omo

Ghana
- 20(c) Forts and Castles in Volta, Greater Accra, Central and Western Regions
- 21(c) Ashante Traditional Buildings

Libyan Arab Jamahiriya
- 22(c) Archaeological Site of Leptis Magna
- 23(c) Archaeological Site of Sabratha
- 24(c) Archaeological Site of Cyrene
- 25(c) Rock-art Sites of Tadrart Acacus
- 26(c) Old Town of Ghadames

Mali
- 27(c) Old Towns of Djenne
- 28(c) Timbuktu
- 29(n/c) Cliff of Bandiagara (Land of the Dogons)

Morocco
- 30(c) Medina of Fez
- 31(c) Medina of Marrakesh
- 32(c) Ksar of Ait-Ben-Haddou

Mozambique
- 33(c) Island of Mozambique

Senegal
- 34(c) Island of Goree

Tanzania, United Republic of
- 35(c) Ruins of Kilwa Kisiwani and Ruins of Songo Mnara

Tunisia
- 36(c) Medina of Tunis
- 37(c) Archaeological Site of Carthage
- 38(c) Amphitheater of El Djem
- 39(c) Punic Town of Kerkuane and Its Necropolis
- 40(c) Medina of Sousse
- 41(c) Kairouan

Zimbabwe
- 42(c) Great Zimbabwe National Monument
- 43(c) Khami Ruins National Monument

Central and Northern Europe

Albania
1(c) Butrinti
Bulgaria
2(c) Boyana Church
3(c) Madara Rider
4(c) Thracian Tomb of Kazanlak
5(c) Rock-hewn Churches of Ivanovo
6(c) Ancient City of Nessebar
7(c) Rila Monastery
8(c) Thracian Tomb of Sveshtari
Croatia
9(c) Old City of Dubrovnik
10(c) Historical Complex of Split with the Palace of Diocletian
Cyprus
11(c) Paphos
12(c) Painted Churches in the TroodosRegion
Czech Republic
13(c) Historic Center of Prague
14(c) Historic Center of Cesky Krumlov
15(c) Historic Center of Telc
16(c) Pilgrimage Church of St. John of Nepomuk at Zelena Hora
17(c) Kutna Hora—The Historical Town Center with the Church of Saint Barbara and the Cathedral of Our Lady at Sedlec
Denmark
18(c) Jelling Mounds, Runic Stones and Church
19(c) Roskilde Cathedral
Finland
20(c) Old Rauma
21(c) Fortress of Suomenlinna
22(c) Petäjävesi Old Church
Georgia
23(c) The City-Museum Reserve of Mtskheta
24(c) Bagrati Cathedral and Gelati
Greece
25(c) Temple of Apollo Epicurius at Bassae
26(c) Archaeological Site of Delphi
27(c) The Acropolis, Athens
28(n/c) Mount Athos
29(n/c) Meteora
30(c) Paleochristian and Byzantine Monuments of Thessalonika
31(c) Archaeological Site of Epidaurus
32(c) Medieval City of Rhodes
33(c) Archaeological Site of Olympia
34(c) Mystras
35(c) Delos
36(c) Monasteries of Daphni, Hossios Lucas and Nea Moni of Chios
37(c) Pythagoreion and Heraion of Samos
Hungary
38(c) Banks of the Danube with District of Buda Castle, Budapest
39(c) Holloko
Hungary/Slovak Republic
40(c) Caves of Aggtelek and Slovak Karst
Lithuania
41(c) Vilnius Historic Center
Luxembourg
42(c) The City of Luxembourg, Its Old Quarters and Fortifications
Macedonia (Former Yugoslav Republic of)
43(n/c) Ohrid Region and Its Lake
Malta
44(c) Hal Saflieni Hypogeum
45(c) City of Valletta
46(c) Ggantija Temples
Netherlands
47(c) Schokland and Its Surroundings
Norway
48(c) Urnes Stave Church
49(c) Bryggen in Bergen
50(c) Roros
51(c) Rock Drawings of Alta
Poland
52(c) Historic Center of Cracow
53(c) Wieliczka Salt Mine
54(c) Auschwitz Concentration Camp
55(c) Historic Center of Warsaw
56(c) Old City of Zamosc
Romania
57(c) Biertan and Its Fortified Church
58(c) Monastery of Horezu
59(c) Churches of Moldavia
Russian Federation
60(c) Historic Center of Saint Petersburg and Related Groups of Monuments
61(c) Kizhi Pogost
62(c) Kremlin and Red Square, Moscow
63(c) Historic Monuments of Novgorod and Surroundings
64(c) Cultural and Historic Ensemble of the Solovetsky Islands
65(c) The White Monuments of Vladimir and Suzdal
66(c) Architectural Ensemble of the Trinity Sergius Lavra in Sergiev Posad
67(c) Church of the Ascension, Kolomenskoye
Slovak Republic
68(c) Vlkolinec
69(c) Spissky Hrad and Its Associated Cultural Monuments
Sweden
70(c) Royal Domain of Drottningholm
71(c) Birka and Hovgarden
72(c) Engelsberg Ironworks
73(c) The Rock Carvings of Tanum
74(c) Skogskyrjogärden
75(c) The Hanseatic Town of Visby
Turkey
76(c) Historic Areas of Istanbul
77(n/c) Goreme National Park and the Rock Sites of Cappadocia
78(c) Great Mosque and Hospital of Divrigi
79(c) Hattusha
80(c) Nemrut Dag
81(c) Xanthos - Letoon
82(n/c) Hierapolis - Pamukkale
83(c) City of Safranbolu
Ukraine
84(c) Saint-Sophia Cathedral and Related Monastic Buildings and Laure of Kievo-Petchersk in Kiev
Yugoslavia
85(c) Stari Ras and Sopocani
86(c) Kotor and Its Gulf
87(c) Studenica Monastery

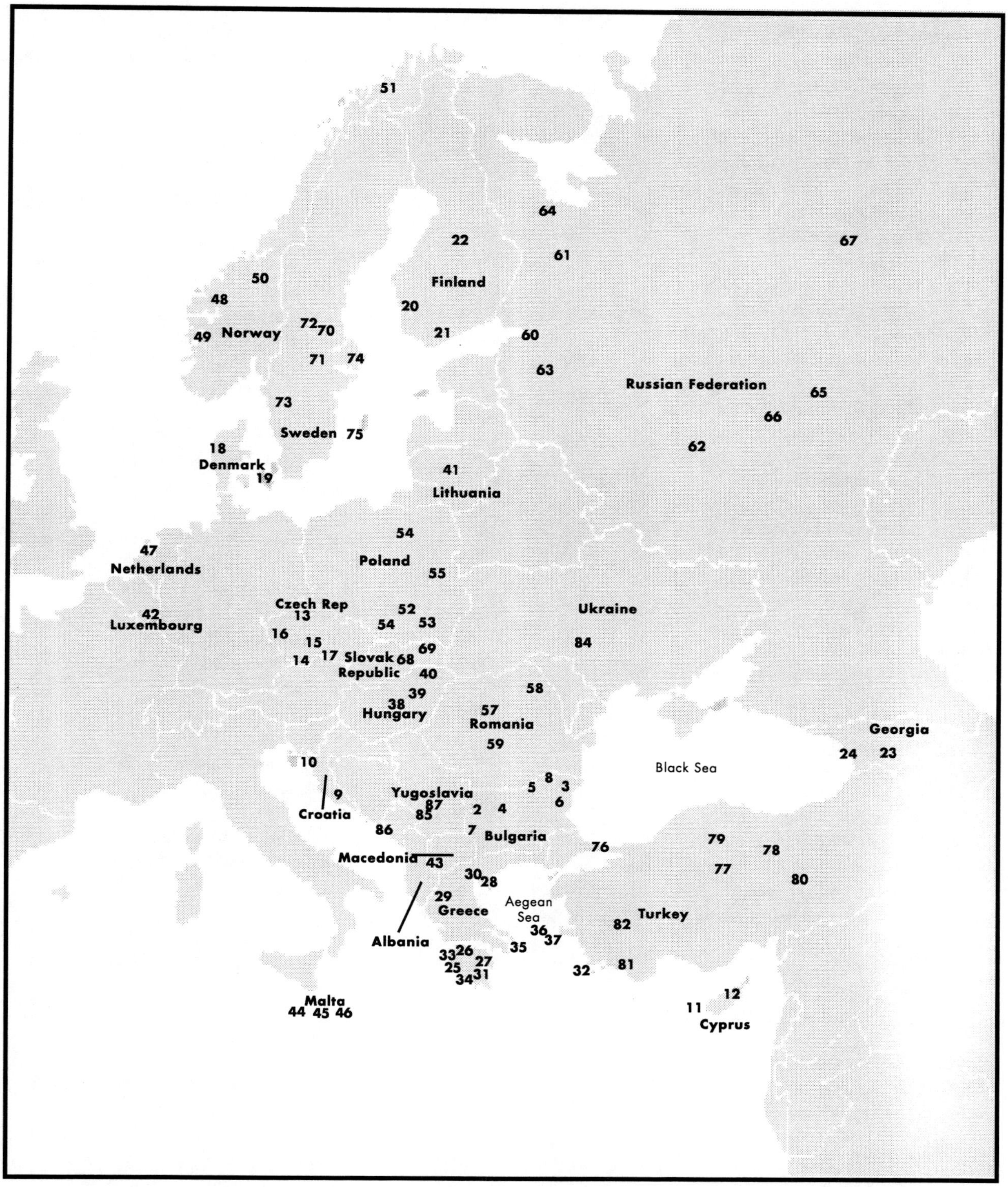
51
64
22
61
67
50
Finland
48
20
72
70
49
Norway
21
60
71
74
63
Russian Federation
65
73
66
Sweden
75
18
62
Denmark
19
41
Lithuania
54
47
Poland
Netherlands
55
Czech Rep
52
Ukraine
42
13
Luxembourg
54
53
16
15
84
69
14
17
Slovak
68
Republic
40
58
39
38
57
Hungary
Romania
Georgia
59
24
23
10
Black Sea
8
5
3
9
Yugoslavia
6
87
2
4
Croatia
85
86
7
Bulgaria
76
79
78
Macedonia
43
77
80
30
28
29
Aegean
Sea
Turkey
Greece
82
36
37
Albania
35
33
26
27
32
81
25
31
34
12
Malta
11
44
45
46
Cyprus

Western Europe

France

1(c) Mont-Saint-Michel and Its Bay
2(c) Chartres Cathedral
3(c) Palace and Park of Versailles
4(c) Basilica and Hill of Vezelay
5(c) Decorated Grottoes of the Vezere Valley
6(c) Palace and Park of Fontainebleau
7(c) Chateau and Estate of Chambord
8(c) Amiens Cathedral
9(c) Roman Theater and Its Surroundings and Triumphal Arch of Orange
10(c) Roman and Romanesque Monuments of Arles
11(c) Cistercian Abbey of Fontenay
12(c) Royal Saltworks of Arc-et-Senans
13(c) Place Stanislas, Place de la Carriere and Place d'Alliance in Nancy
14(c) Church of Saint-Savin-sur-Gartempe
15(c) Pont du Gard (Roman Aqueduct)
16(c) Grande Isle, Strasbourg
17(c) Banks of the Seine, Paris
18(c) Cathedral of Notre-Dame, Former Abbey of Saint-Remi and Palace of Tau, Reims
19(c) Bourges Cathedral
20(c) Historic Center of Avignon

Germany

21(c) Aachen Cathedral
22(c) Speyer Cathedral
23(c) Wurzburg Residence with Court Gardens and Residence Square
24(c) Pilgrimage Church of Wies
25(c) Castles of Augustusburg and Falkenlust at Bruhl
26(c) St. Mary's Cathedral and St. Michael's Church at Hildesheim
27(c) Monuments of Trier
28(c) Hanseatic City of Lubeck
29(c) Palaces and Parks of Potsdam and Berlin
30(c) Abbey and Altenmunster of Lorsch
31(c) Mines of Rammelsberg and the Historic Town of Goslar
32(c) Bamberg
33(c) Maulbronn Monastery Complex
34(c) Collegiate Church, Castle and Old Town of Quedlinburg 35(c) Völkingen Ironworks

Italy

36(c) Rock Drawings in Valcamonica
37(c) Historic Center of Rome
38(c) Church and Dominican Convent of Santa Maria delle Grazie with The Last Supper" by Leonardo da Vinci
39(c) Historic Center of Florence
40(c) Venice and Its Lagoon
41(c) Piazza del Duomo, Pisa
42(c) Historic Center of San Gimignano
43(c) I Sassi di Matera
44(c) Vicenza, City of Palladio
45(c) Historic Center of Siena
46(c) Crespi d'Adda
47(c) Ferrara, City of the Renaissance

Italy/Holy See

48(c) Historic Center of Rome, Properties of the Holy See in That City Enjoying Extraterritorial Rights and San Paolo Fuori le Mura
49(c) Vatican City

Ireland

50(c) Archaeological Ensemble of the Bend of the Boyne

Portugal

51(c) Central Zone of the Town of Angra do Heroismo in the Azores
52(c) Monastery of the Hieronymites and Tower of Belem in Lisbon
53(c) Monastery of Batalha
54(c) Convent of Christ in Tomar
55(c) Historic Center of Evora
56(c) Monastery of Alcobaça
57(c) Cultural Landscape of Sintra

Spain

58(c) Mosque of Cordoba
59(c) The Alhambra and the Generalife, Granada
60(c) Burgos Cathedral
61(c) Monastery and Site of the Escorial, Madrid
62(c) Parque Guell, Palacio Guell and Casa Mila, Barcelona
63(c) Altamira Cave
64(c) Old Town of Segovia and Its Aqueduct
65(c) Churches of the Kingdom of the Asturias
66(c) Old Town of Santiago de Compostela
67(c) Old Town of Avila with Its Extra Muros Churches
68(c) Mudejar Architecture of Teruel
69(c) Historic City of Toledo
70(c) Old Town of Caceres
71(c) Cathedral, Alcazar and Archivo de Indias in Seville
72(c) Old City of Salamanca
73(c) Poblet Monastery
74(c) Archaeological Ensemble of Merida
75(c) Royal Monastery of Santa Maria de Guadalupe
76(c) Route of Santiago de Compostela

Switzerland

77(c) Convent of St. Gall
78(c) Benedictine Convent of St. John at Mustair
79(c) Old City of Berne

United Kingdom

80(c) Durham Castle and Cathedral
81(c) Ironbridge Gorge
82(c) Studley Royal Park including Ruins of Fountains Abbey
83(c) Stonehenge, Avebury and Associated Sites
84(c) Castles and Town Walls of King Edward in Gwynedd
85(c) Blenheim Palace
86(c) City of Bath
87(c) Hadrian's Wall
88(c) Palace of Westminster, Westminster Abbey and Saint Margaret's Church
89(c) Tower of London
90(c) Canterbury Cathedral, St. Augustine's Abbey and St. Martin's Church
91(c) Old and New Towns of Edinburgh

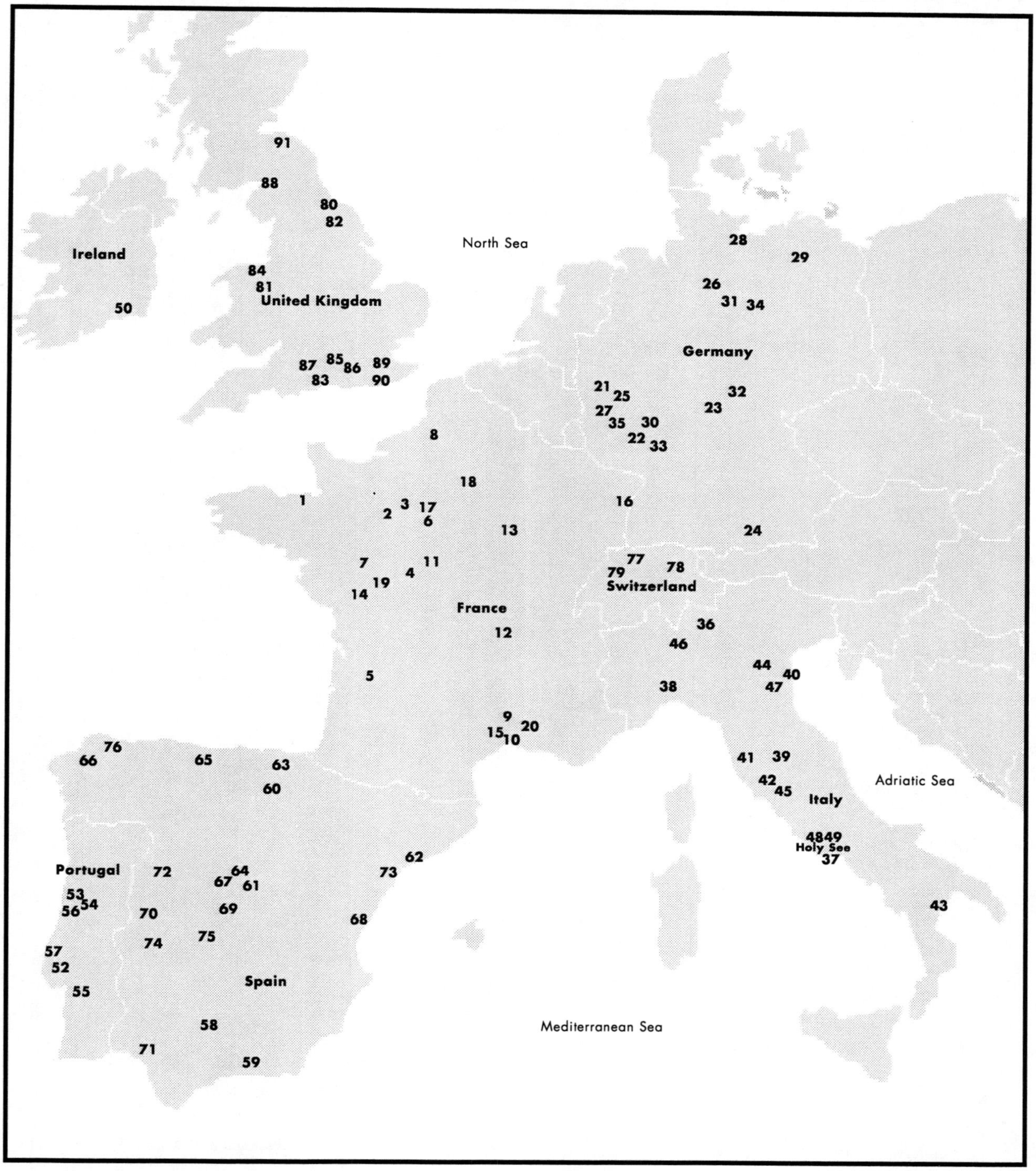
91
88
80
82
Ireland
North Sea
28
29
84
81
United Kingdom
26
31 34
50
Germany
87 85 86 89
83 90
21 25
32
27
23
35 30
22 33
8
18
1
2 3 17
6
16
13
24
7 11
4
77
79 78
19
14
Switzerland
France
12
36
46
5
44 40
47
38
9
15 10 20
76
66
65
63
41 39
60
42 45
Italy
Adriatic Sea
48 49
Holy See
37
62
Portugal
72
64
67 61
73
53 54
56
70
69
68
43
75
57
74
52
Spain
55
58
Mediterranean Sea
71
59

North and Central America

Canada

1(c) L'Anse aux Meadows National Historic Park
2(c) Anthony Island
3(c) Head-Smashed-In Bison Jump Complex
4(c) Historic Area of Quebec
5(c) Lunenburg Old Town

United States of America

6(c) Mesa Verde National Park
7(c) Independence Hall
8(c) Cahokia Mounds State Historic Site
9(c) La Fortaleza and San Juan National Historic Site in Puerto Rico
10(c) Statue of Liberty
11(c) Chaco Culture National Historical Park
12(c) Monticello and University of Virginia, Charlottesville
13(c) Pueblo de Taos

Cuba

14(c) Old Havana and Its Fortifications
15(c) Trinidad and the Valley de los Ingenios

Dominican Republic

16(c) Colonial City of Santo Domingo

El Salvador

17(c) Joya de Ceren Archaeological Site

Guatemala

18(n/c) Tikal National Park
19(c) Antigua Guatemala
20(c) Archaeological Park and Ruins of Quirigua

Haiti

21(c) Citadel, Sans Souci, Ramiers National Historic Park

Honduras

22(c) Maya Site of Copan

Mexico

23(c) Pre-Hispanic City and National Park of Palenque
24(c) Historic Center of Mexico City and Xochimilco
25(c) Pre-Hispanic City of Teotihuacan
26(c) Historic Center of Oaxaca and Archaeological Site of Monte Alban
27(c) Historic Center of Puebla
28(c) Historic Town of Guanajuato and Adjacent Mines
29(c) Pre-Hispanic City of Chichen-Itza
30(c) Historic Centre of Morelia
31(c) El Tajin, Pre-Hispanic City
32(c) Historic Center of Zacatecas
33(c) Rock Paintings of the Sierra de San Francisco
34(c) The Earliest 16th Century Monasteries on the slopes of Popocatepetl

Panama

35(c) Fortifications of Portobelo and San Lorenzo

South America

Argentina & Brazil

1(c) Jesuit Missions of the Guaranis: San Ignacio Mini, Santa Ana, Nuestra Senora de Loreto and Santa Maria la Mayor (Argentina), Ruins of Sao Miguel das Missoes (Brazil)

Bolivia

2(c) City of Potosi

3(c) Jesuit Missions of the Chiquitos

4(c) Historic City of Sucre

Brazil

5(c) Historic Town of Ouro Preto

6(c) Historic Center of the Town of Olinda

7(c) Historic Center of Salvador de Bahia

8(c) Sanctuary of Bom Jesus do Congonhas

9(c) Brasilia

Colombia

10(c) Port, Fortresses and Group of Monuments in Cartagena

11(c) Historic Center of Santa Cruz de Mompox

12(c) National Archaeological Park of Tierradentro

13(c) San Agustin Archaeological Park

Ecuador

14(c) Historic Center of Quito

Paraguay

15(c) Jesuit Missions of La Santisima Trinidad de Parana and Jesus de Tavarangue

Peru

16(c) Historic City of Cuzco

17(n/c) Historic Sanctuary of Macchu Picchu

18(c) Archaeological Site of Chavin

19(c) Chan Chan Archaeological Zone

20(c) Historic Center of Lima

21(n/c) Rio Abiseo National Park

22(c) The Lines and Geoglyphs of Nasca and Pampas de Juma

Uruguay

23(c) Historic Quarter of the City of Colonia del Sacramento

Venezuela

24(c) Coro

The ICOMOS Charter on Cultural Tourism[1] *

Introduction

1 ICOMOS aims to encourage the safeguard and to ensure the conservation and promotion of monuments and sites—that privileged part of the human heritage. In this capacity, it feels directly concerned by the effects—both positive and negative—on said heritage due to the extremely strong development of tourist activities in the world.

2 ICOMOS is conscious that today—even less than heretofore—the isolated effort of anybody, however powerful be it in its own sphere, can validly influence the course of events. This is why it has attempted to participate in joint reflection with the large world and regional organizations which in one capacity or another share in its preoccupations and which are likely to contribute to the implementation of a universal, coherent and efficacious effort.

3 The representatives of these bodies, met in Brussels, Belgium, on 8 and 9 November 1976 at the International Seminar on Contemporary Tourism, have agreed to the following:

The Charter of Cultural Tourism

I. Basic Position

1 Tourism is an irreversible social, human, economic and cultural fact. Its influence in the sphere of monuments and sites is particularly important and can but increase because of the known conditions of that activity's development.

2 Looked at in the perspective of the next twenty-five years, in the context of the phenomena of expansion which may have heavy consequences and which confront the human race, tourism appears to be one of the phenomena likely to exert a most significant influence on man's environment in general and on monuments and sites in particular. In order to remain bearable this influence must be carefully studied, and at all levels be the object of a concerted and effective policy. Without claiming to meet this need in all its aspects, the present approach which is limited to cultural tourism constitutes, it is believed, a positive element in the global solution which is required.

3 Cultural tourism is that form of tourism whose object is, among other aims, the discovery of monuments and sites. It exerts on these last a very positive effect insofar as it contributes—to satisfy its own ends—to their maintenance and protection. This form of tourism justifies in fact the efforts which said maintenance and protection demand of the human community because of the socio-cultural and economic benefits which they bestow on all the populations concerned.

[1]*The charter is currently being revised for ratification at the ICOMOS General Assembly to be held in 1999 in Mexico City.

4 Whatever, however, may be its motivations and the ensuing benefits, cultural tourism cannot be considered separately from the negative, despoiling or destructive effects which the massive and uncontrolled use of monuments and site entails. The respect of the latter, just like the elementary wish to maintain them in a state fit to allow them to play their role as elements of touristic attraction and of cultural education, implies the definition and implementation of acceptable standards.

In any case, with the future in mind, it is the respect of the world, cultural and natural heritage which must take precedence over any other considerations however justified these may be from a social, political or economic point of view.

Such respect cannot be ensured solely by policies regarding the siting of equipment and of guidance of the tourist movements based on the limitations of use and of density which may not be disregarded without impunity.

Additionally one must condemn any siting of tourist equipment or services in contradiction with the prime preoccupation due to the respect we owe to the existing cultural heritage.

II. Basis for Action

Resting on the foregoing,

- the bodies representing tourism, on the one hand, and the protection of the natural and monumental heritage, on the other, deeply convinced that the protection and promotion of the natural and cultural heritage for the benefit of the many cannot be ensured unless it be in an orderly fashion, i.e. by integrating cultural assets into the social and economic objectives which are part of planning of the resources of the states, regions and local communities,

- acknowledge with the greatest interest the measures which each of them states he is prepared to take in his own sphere of influence as expressed in the appendices to the present Declaration,

- appeal to the will of the states to ensure the fast and energetic implementation of the International Convention for the Protection of the World Cultural and Natural Heritage adopted on 16 November 1972 and of the Nairobi Recommendation,

- trust that the World Tourist Organization, fulfilling its aims, and UNESCO in the framework of the Convention mentioned above, shall exert all efforts in cooperation with the signatory bodies and all others who in future may rally to ensure that implementation of the policy which the signatory bodies have defined as the only one able to protect Mankind against the effects of tourism's anarchical growth which would result in the denial of its own objectives.

They express the wish that the states by the means of their administrative structures, of tourist operators' organizations, and users' associations, shall adopt all appropriate measures to facilitate the information and training of persons travelling for tourist purposes inside and out of their country of origin.

Conscious of the acute need which obtains now to change the attitude of the public at large towards the phenomena resulting from the massive development of touristic needs, they express the wish that from school age onwards children and adolescents be educated to understand and respect the monuments, the sites and the cultural heritage and that all written, spoken or visual information media should express to the public the laments of the problems thereby efficaciously contributing to effective universal understanding.

Unanimous in their concern for the protection of the cultural patrimony which is the very basis of international tourism, they undertake to help in the fight initiated on all fronts against the destruction of said heritage by all known sources of pollution; and they appeal to the architects and scientific experts of the whole world so that the most advanced resources of modern technology be used for the protection of monuments.

They recommend that the specialists who shall be called upon to conceive and implement the touristic use of the cultural and the natural heritage should receive training adapted to the multi-faceted nature of the problem, and should be associated from the outset in the programming and performance of the development and tourist equipment plans.

They solemnly declare that their action is to respect and protect the authenticity and diversity of the cultural values in developing regions and countries as in industrialized nations since the fate of Mankind's cultural heritage is of the very same nature everywhere in the face of tourism's likely expansion.

Signatories:

The International Union for the Conservation of Nature and its Resources
The World Federation of Travel Agencies' Association
The International Association of Scientific Experts in Tourism
The International Historic Gardens Committee, ICOMOS
The International Academy of Tourism
The International Bureau for Social Tourism
Europa Nostra
The European Travel Commission
International Federation of Youth Hostels
The International Automobile Federation
International Travel Journalists and Writers Federation
Fondation Van Cle / Van Cle-Stichting
The International Historic Castles Institute
The World Tourism Organization
The International Union of Architects
The International Hotel Association
The International Tourism Alliance

BIBLIOGRAPHY*

Adejuwon, F., "Cultural Heritage as Tourism Product," *Tourist Review*,1985, no. 1, pp. 19-21.

Agnus, J. M. and Meuret, J. P., *Monuments et comptoirs de vente*, Paris, Dept. des Etudes et de la Prospective, Ministere de la Culture, 1988.

Allison, M. T., "Breaking Boundaries and Barriers: Future Directions in Cross-cultural Research," *Leisure Studies*, 1988, vol. 10, pp. 247-259.

Ashley, Robert, "The Visitor Activity Management Process and National Historic Park and Sites Serving the Visitor," *Tourism Recreation Research*, 1989, vol. 14, no. 4 (special issue, 1989), pp. 40-44.

Ashworth, G. J., "Culture and Tourism: Conflict or Symbiosis in Europe?" in *Tourism in Europe*, Praph, W. and Lowery, P. (eds.), London , CAB International, 1994, pp. 13-35.

____________ and Goodall, B., *Marketing Tourism Places*, London and New York, Routledge, 1990.

____________ and Larkham, P. J., *Building a New Heritage: Tourism, Culture, and Identity in the New Europe*, London and New York, Routledge, 1994.

____________ and Turnbridge, J. E., *The Tourist—Historic City*, London, Belhaven, 1990.

Australia Council for the Arts, *Culture on Holiday*, Chippendale, NSW, Australia, Australia Council for the Arts, 1991.

Bady, Jeanne Pierre, *Les Monuments Historiques en France*, (Que Sais-je?), Paris, Presses Universitaires de France, 1985.

Bartoszewicz, W., "The Dynamic Analysis of Tourism," *Problems of Tourism*, Warsaw, Instytut Turystiki, 1988, vol. 11, no. 3, pp. 21-31.

Beeho, Alison J. and Prentice, Richard C., "Evaluating the Experiences and Benefits Gained by Tourists Visiting a Socio-Industrial Heritage Museum: An Application of ASEB Grid Analysis to Blists Hill Open-Air Museum, The Ironbridge Gorge Museum, United Kingdom, *Museum Management and Curatorship*, 1995, vol. 14, no. 3, pp. 229-251.

Belk, R. W., "Symbolic Consumption of Art and Culture," in *Artist and Cultural Consumers*, Shaw, D. V. (ed.), Akron, Ohio, University of Akron, 1987, pp. 168-178.

Bird, Jon; Curtis, Barry; Putnam, Tim; Robertson, George; and Tickner, Lisa, *Mapping the Futures. Local Cultures, Global Change*, London and New York, Routledge, 1993.

Bitter, M., "Singapore: The Street of Happy Death," *Vue Touristique*, 1989, no. 79, pp. 12-14.

Bochner, S., *Cultures in Contact*, Oxford, U.K., Pergamon Press, 1982.

Boniface, Priscilla, *Managing Quality Cultural Tourism*, London and New York, Routledge, 1995.

* Published before July 1996.

_______________ and Fowler, Peter J., *Heritage and Tourism in "The Global Village,"* London and New York, Routledge, 1993.

Bonink, C. and Richards, G., *Cultural Tourism in Europe*, ATLAS [European Association for Tourism and Leisure Education] Research Report, London, University of North London, 1992.

Bouquet M. and Winter, M., *Who From Their Labours Rest? Conflict and Practice in Rural Tourism*, Aldershot, Hants, U.K., Gower Publishing Co., 1987.

Bowes, Robert G., "Tourism and Heritage—A New Approach to the Product," *Tourism Recreation Research*, 1989, vol. 14, no.4, pp. 30-35.

British Tourist Authority (BTA), *The Economic Significance of Tourism within the European Community*, London, 1983.

_____________________ *Heritage 1984*, Report of the 1983 Conference on Tourism, London, BTA.

Brougham, J. E., *The Social and Cultural Impact of Tourism: A Case Study in Sleat, Isle of Skye*, Edinburgh, Scottish Tourist Board, 1977.

Butler, R. W. and Waldbrook, L. A., "A New Planning Tool: The Tourism Opportunity Spectrum," *Journal of Tourism Studies*, 1991, vol. 2, pp. 2-14.

Butler, Richard and Pearce, Douglas, *Change in Tourism: People, Places, Processes*, London and New York, Routledge, 1995.

Bystrzanowski, Julian (ed.), *Tourism as a Factor of Change: A Sociocultural Study*, Vienna, The Vienna Centre, 1989.

Cameron, C. M., "Cultural Tourism and Urban Revitalization," *Tourism Recreation Research*, 1989, vol. 14, no. 1, pp. 23-32.

Canan, P. and Hennessy, M., "The Growth Machine, Tourism, and the Selling of Culture," *Sociological Perspectives*, 1989, vol. 32, no. 2, pp. 227-243.

Causi, M. and Gorelli, S., "Dilemma e paradosso dei beni culturali e delle citta d'arte," *Politica del Turismo*, Rimini, Italy, Maggioli Editore, 1987, vol. 4, no. 3.

Cohen, E., "The Impact of Tourism on the Physical Environment," *Annals of Tourism Research*, 1978, vol. 5, no. 2, pp. 215-237.

Colbert, Francois, "L'impact economique des activites a caractere culturel," (lecture at a conference on *Journee sur le tourisme et les Arts*, Ecole des Hautes Etudes Commerical de Montreal, Nov. 24-25, 1983), pp. 1-10.

Consumers Association of Penang, *See the World While It Lasts*, 1985, Malaysia.

Cooper, C. P., *Progress in Tourism, Recreation and Hospitality Management*, London, Belhaven Press, 1989.

Corna Pellegrini, Giacomo, *Esplorando Polis: Itinerari de Geografia Umana*, Milan, Edizioni Unicopli, 1989.

Cossons, N., "Heritage Tourism: Trends and Tribulations," *Tourism Management*, 1989, vol. 10, no. 3, pp. 192-194.

Dalibard, Jacques, "Has Cultural Tourism Become a Trivial Pursuit?" *Canadian Heritage*, vol. 11, 1985, no. 1, pp. 2-5.

Davidson, Suzanne (ed.), *Cultural Tourism: Making It Work, Planning and Marketing for Cultural Tourism*, Sydney, Australia, Museum Association of Australia and the Museum Studies Unit, University of Sydney, 1991.

DeCambra, H., "Alternative Tourism," *Contours*, 1988, vol. 3, no. 8, pp. 16-21.

Dickens, Roy S. and Hill, Carole E. (eds.), *Cultural Resources-Planning and Management*, (Social Impact Assessment Series, no. 2), Boulder, Colo., Westview Press, 1978.

Din, K. H., "Social and Cultural Impacts of Tourism," *Annals of Tourism Research*, 1988, vol. 15, no. 4, pp. 563-566.

Dogan, Hasan, "Forms of Adjustment: Sociocultural Impacts of Tourism," *Annals of Tourism Research*, 1989, vol.16, no. 2. pp. 216-236.

Dromard, C., "Tourism and Heritage: Reconciliation?" *Leisure Recreation and Tourism Abstracts*, 1988, no. 92, pp. 9-10.

Drost, Anne, "Developing Sustainable Tourism for World Heritage Sites," *Annals of Tourism Research*, 1996, vol. 23, no.2. pp. 179-184.

Edington, J. M. and Edington, M. A., *Ecology Recreation and Tourism*, Cambridge, U.K., Cambridge University Press, 1986.

Eldergill, M. A., "Identification of Traditional Values in Micronesia," *Annals of Tourism Research*, 1988, vol. 15, no. 3, pp. 446-448.

Elliot, James, *The Management and Politics of Tourism*, London and New York, Routledge, 1996.

English Tourist Board, *English Cathedrals and Tourism: Problems and Opportunities*, London, 1979.

Evans, N. H., "The Tourism of Indian California: A Neglected Legacy," *Annals of Tourism Research*, 1986, vol. 13, no. 3, pp. 435-450.

Farrell, B. H. and McLellan, R. W., "Tourism and the Physical Environment," *Annals of Tourism Research*, 1987, vol. 14, no. 1, pp. 1-16.

Fawcett, Jane (ed.), Seminar papers on "Tourist Wear and Tear," UK/ICOMOS, 1989.

_________ (ed.), Papers from "Heritage and Tourism: ICOMOS European Conference," UK/ICOMOS, 1990.

_________ (ed.), "Surveys of Historic Floors of Cathedrals and Greater Churches," UK/ICOMOS, 1991.

_________ (ed.), Seminar papers on "Management of World Heritage Sites," UK/ICOMOS, 1992.

Fowler, Peter, *The Past in Contemporary Society. Then, Now*, London and New York, Routledge, 1992.

Fragola, Umberto, "Tourisme et qualite de la vie," *Tourist Review*, 1985, no. 1, pp. 7-8.

_____________ "Enjoyment by Tourists of the Cultural Resources of Social Customs," *Rassegna di studi turistica*, 1986, vol. 6.

Furnham, A., "Tourism and Culture Shock," *Annals of Tourism Research*, 1984, vol. 11, no. 1, pp. 41-57.

Garay, M., *Le Tourisme Culturel en France*, Paris, La Documentation Francaise, 1980.

GEATTE (Groupement d'Etude et d'Assistance pour l'Amenagement du Territoire, le Tourisme et l'Environnement), *Le Tourisme Culturel en Europe*, Luxembourg and UNIPUB, Lanham, Md., USA, Office des Publications Officielles des Communautes Europeennes, 1994.

Gomez, Venancio B., "Tourisme rural en Espagne et patrimoine bati," *Tourist Review*, 1985, no. 1, pp. 21-23.

Greffe, X., *Crise des villes mediterraneenes et tourisme culturel*, Paris, Colloque de Palerme, OECD, 1989.

Grodecky, Louis, "L'Usure du Patrimoine: Deux Exemples [Lascaux]," *Revue de l'Art*, 1980, vol. 80, no. 49, pp. 89-95.

Grodwohl, M., "The Eco-Museum—Curriculum Vitae," *Leisure, Recreation and Tourism Abstracts*, 1988, no. 92, pp. 21-23.

Gyte, D. M., "Tourist Cognition of Destination: An Exploration of Techniques of Measurement and Representation of Images of Tunisia," *Trent Working Papers in Geography*, 1987.

________ "Repertory Grid Analysis of Image Destinations: British Tourists in Mallorca," *Trent Working Papers in Geography*, Nottingham, U.K., 1988.

Hall, Colin Michael, *Tourism and Politics: Policy, Power and Place*, New York, Wiley, 1994.

Hall, M. and Zeppel, H., "Cultural and Heritage Tourism: the New Grand Tour?" *Historic Environment*, 1990, vol. 7, nos. 3 and 4, pp. 86-98.

Harris, F., "From the Industrial Revolution to the Heritage Industry," *Geographical Magazine*, 1989, vol. 61, no. 5, pp. 38-42.

Hartman, R., "Dachau: Tourism to the Memorial Site and Museum of the Former Concentration Camp," *Tourism Recreation Research*, 1989, vol. 14, no. 1, pp. 41-47.

Heeley, John, "Heritage and Tourism: An Overview," *Heritage Tourism and Leisure*, Edinburgh, 1989.

Hendon, W. S., *Economics and Historic Preservation*, Akron, Ohio, University of Akron, 1983.

Henry, O., "Tourism and Culture—An Announcement of Marriage," *Leisure, Recreation and Tourism Abstracts*, 1988, no. 92, pp. 7-8.

Herbert, D. T., Prentice, R. C., and Thomas, C. J. (eds.), *Heritage Sites: Strategies for Marketing and Development*, Avebury, Aldershot, 1989.

Herron, Nancy L. (ed.), *The Leisure Literature: A Guide to Sources in Leisure Studies, Fitness, Sports, and Travel*, Englewood, Colo., Libraries Unlimited, 1992.

Hewison, R., *The Heritage Industry: Britain in a Climate of Decline*, London, Methuen, 1986.

Hollinshead, Keith, "Cultural Tourism," *Annals of Tourism Research*, 1990, vol. 17, no. 2, pp. 292-294.

Horne, D., *The Great Museum: The Re-Representation of History*, London, Pluto Press, 1984.

________ *The Intelligent Tourist*, McMahone Point, New South Wales, Australia, Margaret Gee Holdings, 1992.

Honeyborne, David B., "Weathering and Decay Phenomena," in *Conservation of Building and Decorative Stone*, London, Butterworth-Heinemann, 1990, vol. 1, pp. 153-184.

Hughes, H. L., "Culture as a Tourist Resource—A Theoretical Consideration," *Tourism Management*, 1987, vol. 8, no. 3, pp. 205-216.

__________ "Tourism and the Arts: A Potentially Destructive Relationship," *Tourism Management*, 1989, vol 10, no. 2, pp. 97-99.

Hunter, Colin and Green, Howard, *Tourism and the Environment: A Sustainable Relationship?* London and New York, Routledge, 1995.

ICOMOS Australia, "Cultural Heritage and Tourism," in *Historic Environment*, ICOMOS/Australia, 1990, vol. 7, nos. 3 and 4.

ICOMOS Canada, *Momentum*, (thematic issue devoted to cultural tourism), 1994, vol. 3, no. 3.

Inskeep, Edward, *National and Regional Tourism Planning: Methodologies and Case Studies*, London and New York, Routledge, in collaboration with The World Tourism Organization, 1994.

Ioualalen, Suzy, "Overall Expectation of Conference," *1st International Conference on Cultural Tourism; Defining a Sense of Place*, Miami, unpublished report, 1989.

Irish Tourist Board, *Inventory of Cultural Tourism Resources in the Member States and Assessment of Methods Used to Promote Them*, Brussels, European Commission DG VII, 1988.

Jafari, J., "On Domestic Tourism," *Tourism Recreation Research*, 1987, vol. 12, no. 1, pp. 29-31.

Kaplan, Marilyn E., "Fire Protection at Remote Historic Sites," *International Symposium on Fire Protection of Historic Buildings and Towns*, Larsen, Knut Einart and Marstein, Nils (eds.), Norway, Tapir Publishers, 1992, pp. 33-52.

Kia, B. and Williams, B. C., "Saving Sana-a," *Geographical Magazine*, 1989, vol. 61, no. 5, pp. 32-36.

Kindley, A., "The Charter for Cultural Tourism," *Leisure Recreation and Tourism Abstracts*, 1989, vol. 2b, no. 6, p. 12.

Kirshenblatt-Gimblett, Barbara, *Destination Culture*, Los Angeles, Calif.: University of California Press, 1997.

________________»Tourism and Heritage» in *Traditions and Tourism:The Good, the Bad, and the Ugly*, Faine, Susan, (ed.), Melbourne, Australia, Victorian Folklife Association, 1994, pp. 1-11.

_______________ «Theorizing Heritage,» *Ethnomusicology* , 1995, vol. 39, pp. 367-380.

_______________ «Heritage: A New Mode of Cultural Production,» *Tourism & Travel Review* (Sydney),
1994, vol. 3, pp. 8-9.

_______________ «Destination Museum: Heritage, Museums and Tourism,» in *Destination Museum: Issues of Heritage, Museums and Tourism*—Seminar Transcript, Wellington, New Zealand, August 15, 1994, Wellington, New Zealand: Museum Directors Federation of Aotearoa/New Zealand Inc., 1994, pp. 4-65.

_______________ and Bruner, Edward M., «Maasai on the Lawn: Tourist Realism in East Africa.» *Cultural Anthropology*, 1994, vol. 9, pp. 435-470.

_______ and Bruner, Edward M, «Tourism,» *Folklore, Cultural Performances, and Popular Entertainments*, Bauman, Richard (ed.), reprinted from *International Encyclopedia of Communication*, 1991.

Krippendorf, Jost, *The Holiday Makers:Understanding the Impact of Leisure and Travel*, Oxford, Butterworth-Heineman, 1987.

Kramer, Dieter and Lutz, Ronald (eds.), *Tourismus-Kultur, Kultur-Tourismus*, Kulturwissenschaftliche Horizonte, Band 1. Munster, Lit, 1993.

Krumbein, Wolfang, "Graffiti and Anti-Graffiti: An Appraisal," *Conservation of Architectural Surfaces: Stones and Wall Covering*, Venice, Il Cardo, 1993, pp. 61-67.

Laarman, J. G. and Perdue, R. R., "Science Tourism in Costa Rica," *Annals of Tourism Research*, 1989, vol. 16, no. 2, pp. 205-215.

Lanquar, Robert G., "Nouveau Patrimoine, Nouveau Tourism," *Tourist Review*, 1984, no. 4, pp. 12-16.

Lea, John, *Tourism and Development in the Third World*, London and New York, Routledge, 1988.

Leisure Studies Association, Papers of Conference, "Tourism and Leisure: Towards the Millennium—April 1994, Glasgow," *Leisure Studies*, 1995, vol. 51.

Lennon, J., "The Tensions of Making Use of Our Cultural Heritage," *Historic Environment*, 1990, vol. 7, nos. 3 and 4, pp. 55-60.

Leong, Wai Teng, "Culture and the State—Manufacturing Traditions for Tourism," *Critical Studies in Mass Communication*, 1989, vol. 6, no. 4, pp. 355-375.

Lowenthal, David, *Possessed by the Past: The Heritage Crusade and the Spoils of History*, New York, Free Press, 1996.

MacCannell, Dean, "Reconstructed Ethnicity: Tourism and Cultural Diversity in Third World Communities," *Annals of Tourism Research*, 1984, vol. 11, no. 3, pp. 375-391.

_____________ *Empty Meeting Grounds: The Tourist Papers*, London and New York, Routledge, 1992.

_____________ *The Tourist: A New Theory of the Leisure Class*, New York, Schocken, 1976/1989.

Madaumier, J., "Cultural Tourism," *Leisure Recreation and Tourism, Abstracts*, 1988, no. 92, pp. 2- 5.

Machin, A., "Outlook Unsettled? A Personal View of Heritage," *Heritage Outlook* (London, Civic Trust), 1988, vol. 8, no. 4, pp. 78-79.

Makens, J. C., "The Importance of U.S. Historic Sites and Visitor Attractions," *Journal of Travel Research*, 1987, vol. 25, no. 3, pp. 8-12.

Malempre, George, "Le tourisme comme industrie culturelle," *Tourist Review*, 1982, no. 2, pp. 2-5.

Medlik, S., "Trends in International Tourism: Past, Present and Future," *European Workshop on Cultural Tourism in Mediterranean Islands*, Malta, 1988.

________ *Dictionary of Travel, Tourism and Hospitality*, Oxford, Butterworth-Heinemann, 1993.

Mendoza, L., "Tourism and Heritage," *Leisure Management*, 1986, vol. 6, no. 11, pp. 30-32.

Michaud, Jean-Luc, *Tourismes: Chance pour l'Economie, Risque pour les Societes?* (Nouvelle Encyclopedie Diderot), Paris, Presses Universitaires de France, 1992.

Millar, Sue, "Heritage Management for Heritage Tourism," *Tourism Management*, 1989, vol. 10, pp. 9-14.

Misiani, C.R., "Tourism Itineraries as a Focus of Integration Between Tourism and Cultural Resources," *Rassegna di studi turistica*, 1986, no. 6.

Moulin, Claude, "Plans for Ecological and Cultural Tourism Involving Participation of Local Populations and Associations," *Tourism Planning and Development Issues*, Washington, D.C., 1980, pp. 192-212.

_____________ "Touristic Leisure, an Element of Mixing and Cultural Development or Hopes Rediscovered," *Tourist Review*, 1985, no. 2, pp. 2-5.

_____________ "Do We Really Need a Supermarket Type of Tourism?" *Journal of the Canadian Hospitality Institute*, 1985, vol. 13, no. 4, pp. 69-77.

_____________ "Education, Tourisme et Tiers Monde," *Canadian Journal of Development Studies*, 1987, vol. 8, no. 2, pp. 251-260.

_____________ "Cultural Tourism Theory," *Planning for Cultural Tourism*, University of Calgary, Canada, 1989, pp. 43-61.

_____________ "Patrimoine et Tourisme: developper un sens de lieu," *Tourist Review*, 1989, no. 3, pp. 12-16.

_____________ "Cultural Heritage and Tourism Evolution," *Historic Environment*, 1990, vol. 7, nos. 3 and 4, pp. 82-85.

Munsters, W., *Cultuurtoerisme*, Apeldoorn, The Netherlands, Garant, 1994.

Munt, I., "The Other Postmodern Tourism—Culture, Travel and the New Middle Classes," *Theory, Culture and Society*, 1994, vol. 11, no. 3, pp. 101-123.

Murphy, P., *Tourism: A Community Approach*, London, Methuen, 1985.

Mycklebust, D., "Tourism and the Heritage: Conflict or Cooperation?" *Norway: A Cultural Heritage, Monuments and Sites*, (ICOMOS bulletin, no. 7), Oslo, Norway, 1987, pp. 345-359.

Nora, P., *Les lieux de memoire*, vol. 2, Paris, Gallimard, 1986.

Nureddin, M. A. H., "Museums, Civilization and Development," in *Encounter of Arab Museum Professionals. Amman, Jordan. April 26-29, 1994*. Paris, ICOM, 1994-5.

O'Reilly, A. M., "Tourism Carrying Capacity: Concept and Issues," *Tourism Management*, 1986, vol. 7, no. 4., pp. 254-258.

Patin, V. *Les Nouvelles Image du Patrimoine et la Consommation Touristique*, Colloque Tourime et Patrimoine, Avignon, 1987.

_______ "Valorisation touristique du patrimoine cultural," *Developpement Cultural*, 1989, vol. 83.

_______ and Bobbio, Luigi, "Le politiche dei beni culturali in Europa," *Il Mulino*, Bologne, 1992.

_______ and Croize, J. C., "Valorisation touristique du patrimoine bati," Congres del'AIEST [International Association of Scientific Experts in Tourism], Prague, 1984.

Pearce, D., "Tourism and Environmental Research, a Review," *International Journal of Environmental Studies*, 1985, vol. 25, no. 4, pp. 247-255.

Pearce, P. L., *The Social Psychology of Tourist Behaviour*, Oxford, Pergamon Press, 1982.

Peleggi, Maurizio, "National Heritage and Global Tourism in Thailand," *Annals of Tourism Research*, 1996, vol. 23, no. 2, pp. 432-448.

Picard, M., "From 'Cultural Tourism' to 'Tourist Culture'," *Leisure Recreation and Tourism Abstracts*, 1989, vol. 10, no. 2, pp. 35-52.

Pigram, J. J., "Environmental Implications of Tourism Development," *Annals of Tourism Research*, 1980, vol. 7, pp. 554-583.

Polacek, M. and Aroch, R., "Analysis of Cultural Sights' Attractiveness for Tourism," *Tourist Review*, 1984, vol. 4, pp. 17-18.

Prentice, Richard, *Tourism and Heritage Attractions*. London and New York, Routledge, 1993.

____________ "Motivations of the Heritage Consumer in the Leisure Market. An Application of the Manning-Haas Demand Hierarchy," *Leisure Sciences*, 1993, vol. 15, no. 4, pp. 273-290.

____________ "Perceptual Deterrents to Visiting Museums and Other Heritage Attractions," *Museum Management and Curatorship*, 1994, vol. 13, pp. 264-279.

____________ and Light, D., "Current Issues in Interpretative Provision at Heritage Sites," in *Tourism: The State of the Art*, Seaton, A.V. et al. (eds.), London, Wiley, 1994, pp. 204-221.

Raffestin, Claude, "Le role de la ville d'art dans l'avenement d'une economie de la contemplation," *Cahiers de geographie du Quebec*, 1988, vol. 32, no. 85, pp. 61-66.

Richards, Greg, "Cultural Tourism in Europe," *Progress in Tourism, Recreation and Hospitality Management*, 1993, vol. 5, pp. 99-115.

____________ "Developments in European Cultural Tourism," in *Tourism: The State of the Art*, Seaton, A.V. et al. (eds.), London, Wiley, 1994, pp. 366-376.

____________ "Production and Consumption of European Cultural Tourism," *Annals of Tourism Research*, 1996, vol. 23, no. 2. pp. 261-283.

Rifkind, C., "Cultural Tourism: A New Opportunity for the Industrial City?" *Environmental Comment*, Washington, D.C., Urban Land Institute, 1981, pp. 4-7.

Robinson, Mike, Evans, Nigel, and Callaghan, Paul, *Tourism and Culture: Towards the 21st Century*, Conference Proceedings, University of Northumbria at Newcastle (4 vols.: Tourism and Culture: Image, Identity and Marketing; Culture as the Tourist Product; Managing Cultural Resources for the Tourist; Tourism and Cultural Change), Sunderland, U.K., Centre for Travel and Tourism in association with Business Education Publishers, Ltd., 1996.

Romeril, M., "Tourism and Conservation in the Channel Islands," *Tourism Management*, 1985, vol. 6, no. 1, pp. 43-49.

Sagi, M., "Motivational Background of Cultural Activities in Leisure," *Leisure Studies*, 1986, vol. 5, no. 1, pp. 103-108.

Saldanha, M., "Carnival: the Epitome of Tourism in Brazil," *Contours*, 1987, vol. 3, no. 3, pp. 5-7.

Scherrer, Christian P., *Tourismuskritik als Zivilisationskritik: Grundrisse der Kritik der Touristischen Bewegung*, 3 vols., Bern, Scorpion, 1983.

Second International Congress on Architectural Conservation and Town Planning, *Conservation and Tourism*, Basel, Switzerland, April 1-4, 1985, pp. 1-6.

Shafernich, S.M., "On-Site Museums, Open-Air Museums, Museum Villages and Living History Museums," *Museum Management and Curatorship*, 1993, vol. 12, pp. 43-61.

Shepstone, T., "Future Tourism Projects," *Tourism Management*, 1987, vol. 8, no. 2, pp. 131-133.

Silberberg, T., "Cultural Tourism and Business Opportunities for Museums and Heritage Sites," *Tourism Management*, 1995, vol. 16, no. 5, pp. 361-365.

Sindiyo, D. M. and Pertet, F. N., "Tourism and Its Impact on Wildlife in Kenya," *UNDP: Industry and Environment*, 1984, vol. 7, no. l, New York, United Nations.

Smith, Valene L., *Hosts and Guests: The Anthropology of Tourism*, Philadelphia, University of Pennsylvania, 1977/1989.

_______________ "Tourism in the Socio-Cultural Environment," *Tourism Recreation Research*, 1989, vol. 14, no. 1, pp. 1-3.

_______________ *Pilgrimage and Tourism: The Quest in Guest*, special issue of *Annals of Tourism Research*, 1992, vol. 19, no. 1. pp. 1-121.

____________ and Eadington, William R., *Tourism Alternatives*, (papers presented at August 1989 meeting of the International Academy for the Study of Tourism in Zakapone, Poland), Philadelphia, University of Pennsylvania Press, 1992.

Srisang, K., "Paradise Threatened," *Contours*, 1987, vol. 3, no. 4, pp. 3-6.

Stirling, A., "Too Many Visitors?" *ICOMOS Information*, 1990, no. 3, pp. 26-33.

Stringer, P., "Studies in the Socio-Environmental Psychology of Tourism," *Annals of Tourism Research*, 1984, vol. 11, no. 1., pp. 41-58.

Tabata, R. and Cherem, G. (eds.), *Proceedings of the Third Global Congress of Heritage Interpretation International*, Chicago and Hawai, University of Chicago Press and The University of Hawaii Press, 1992.

Theobald, William (ed.), *Global Tourism: The Next Decade*, Oxford, Butterworth-Heinemann, 1994.

Theuns, H. L., "Appropriate Tourism for the Third World: A Bibliography in the Sociocultural Dimension—1963-1984," *Tourism Recreation Research*, 1987, vol. 12, no. 2, pp. 55-64.

Thorburn, A., "Marketing Cultural Heritage: Does It Work within Europe?" *Travel and Tourism Analyst* (London), Dec., 1986, pp. 39-48.

Thurot, J. M. and Thurot, G., "The Ideology of Class and Tourism: Confronting the Discourse of Advertising," *Annals of Tourism Research*, 1983, vol. 10, no. 1, pp. 173-189.

Tighe, Anthony, "Cultural Tourism in the USA," *Tourism Management*, 1985, vol. 6, no. 4, pp. 234-251.

____________ "The Arts/Tourism Partnership," *Travel Industry Association of America*, Washington, D.C., Jan. 1985, pp. 1-23.

Tribe, John, *The Economics of Leisure and Tourism*, Oxford and Boston, Butterworth-Heinemann, 1995.

UNESCO, "Preservation of Sites, Monuments, and Traditional Architecture: Monuments and Traditional Architecture," *Annals of Tourism Research*, 1976, vol. 4, no. 2, pp. 96-101.

Urry, John, *The Tourist Gaze: Leisure and Travel in Contemporary Societies*, London, Sage Publications, 1990.

_________ "Cultural Change and Contemporary Tourism," *Leisure Studies*, 1994, vol. 13, pp. 1-6.

Uzzell, D. L., "A Structuralist Alternative to Tourism Marketing," *Annals of Tourism Research*, 1984, vol. 16, no. 3, pp. 79-99.

_________ "The Interpretive Experience," in *Ethnoscopes, Volume II: Environmental Policy, Assessment and Communication*, Canter, D., Krampen, M., and Stea, D. (eds.), Aldershot, Hants, U.K., Gower Publishing Co., 1988.

_________ *Heritage Interpretation: Volume I: The Natural and Built Environment*, London, Belhaven Press, 1989.

_________ *Heritage Interpretation: Volume II: The Visitor Experience*, London, Belhaven Press, 1989.

van den Berghe, Pierre, *The Quest for the Other: Ethnic Tourism in San Cristóbal, Mexico*, Seattle and London, University of Washington Press, 1994.

Var, T., Shluter, R., Ankomak, P. and Lee, T. H., "Tourism and World Peace: the Case in Argentina," *Annals of Tourism Research*, 1989, vol. 16, no. 3, pp. 431- 433.

Vukonic, B. and Tkalac D., "Tourism and Urban Revitalization: A Case Study of Porce, Yugoslavia," *Annals of Tourism Research*, 1984, vol. 11, no. 4, pp. 591- 605.

Wall, G., "An International Perspective on Historic Sites, Recreation and Tourism," *Recreation Research Review*, 1989, vol. 14, no. 4, p. 10-14.

Weightman, B. A., "Third World Tour Landscapes," *Annals of Tourism Research*, 1987, vol. 14, no. 2, pp. 227-239.

Weiler, Betty and Hall, Collin Michael (eds.), *Special Interest Tourism*, London, Belhaven, 1992.

Welch, G., Tauke, M., and Glover, G., "Multicultural Human Resource Management," *Hospitality, Education and Research Journal*, 1988, vol. 12, no. 2, pp. 337-345.

Wood, K. and House, S., *The Good Tourist*, London, Mandarin, 1991.

Wood, R. E., "Ethnic Tourism, the State and Cultural Change in South-East Asia," *Annals of Tourism Research*, 1984, vol. 11, no. 3, pp. 353-374.

World Bank, *Tourism, Passport to Development?*, Washington, D.C., 1979.

World Commission on Environment and Development, *Our Common Future*, Oxford and New York, Oxford University Press, 1987.

World Tourism Organization, *Report of the Secretary General 1984-1985 on State's Role in Protecting Culture as a Factor in Tourism Development*, Madrid, WTO, 1985.

______________________ *Tourism to the Year 2000: Qualitative Aspects Affecting Global Growth. A Discussion Paper. Executive Summary*, Madrid, WTO, 1991.

______________________ *Situation of Tourism in the Countries Formerly Belonging to COMECON*, Madrid, WTO, 1993.

Yale, P., *From Tourist Attractions to Heritage Tourism*, Huntingdon, U.K., ELM Publications, 1991.

International Tourism Periodicals

The following periodicals may be of particular interest and use to a site administrator:

Annals of Tourism Research
A social sciences quarterly journal (summaries in French) begun in 1974. Editor's address: University of Wisconsin-Stout, Department of Habitational Resources, Menomonie, Wisconsin 54751, USA. Available from Pergamon Press, Inc., Journals Division, Maxwell House, Fairview Park, Elmsford, New York, N.Y. 10523, U.S.A..

Cahiers du Tourisme
Published by Universite d'Aix-Marseille III (Universite de Droit, d'Economie et des Sciences), Centre des Hautes Etudes Touristiques, Fondation Vasarely, 1 Av. Marcel Pagnol, 13090 Aix-en-Provence. Publishes irregularly four series: France, Etranger, Recherche Fondamentale et Appliquee-Methodologie, Legislation.

International Tourism Reports
Quarterly begun in 1971 published by Economist Intelligences Unit, 111 W. 57th St., New York, NY 10019. Formerly *International Tourism Quarterly.*

Journal of Sustainable Tourism
Quarterly journal begun in 1993, published by Multilingual Matters Ltd., Frankfurt Lodge, Clevedon Hall, Victoria Rd., Clevedon, Avon BS21 7SJ, England.

Journal of Tourism Studies
Published by James Cook University of North Queensland, Department of Tourism, Townsville, Qld. 4811, Australia.

Journal of Travel & Tourism Marketing
Quarterly journal begin in 1992. Published by Haworth Press, Inc., 10 Alice St., Binghamton, NY 13904-1580, U.S.A.

Journal of Travel Research
Quarterly journal begun in 1962 (formerly *Travel Research Bulletin*). Produced by and available from Travel and Tourism Research Association, Business Research Division, University of Colorado, Graduate School of Business Administration, Boulder, Colorado 80309, U.S.A.

Revue de l'Academie Internationale du Tourisme
Quarterly published since 1951 by Academie Internationale du Tourisme, 4 rue des Iris, Monte Carlo, Monaco.

Tourism Management
Quarterly journal begun in 1980. Published by Butterworth Scientific Ltd., P.O. Box 63, Westbury House, Bury St., Guilford, Surrey GU2 5BH, England. Subscription address: Westbury Subscription Services, P.O. Box 101, Sevenoaks, Kent TN 15 8PL, England.

Tourism Policy and International Tourism in OECD Member Countries
Published by Organization for Economic Cooperation and Development, 2 rue Andre-Pascal, 75775 Paris Cedex 16, France.

Tourism Recreation Research

Semiannual publication plus special issues begun in 1976. Published by Centre for Tourism Research, A-965/6 Indira Nagar, Lucknow 226016, India.

Tourist Review/Revue de Tourisme/Zeitschrift für Fremdenverkehr
Quarterly published by the International Association of Scientific Experts in Tourism begun in 1946. Available from Varnbülstr. 19, CH -9000, St. Gallen, Switzerland.

The Travel and Tourism Index
Published in Laie, Hawaii: Business Division, Brigham Young University—Hawaii Campus. Box 1773, Laie, HI 96762.

World Tourism Organization: Tourist Bibliography
Published three times per year, including annual Legislation Supplement, by World Tourism Organization, Capitán Haya 42, 208020 Madrid, Spain. Text in English, French and Spanish.

Selected International and Regional Organizations Related to Cultural Tourism

Caribbean Tourism Organization (CTO)
20 East 46th Street
New York, N.Y. 10017 U.S.A.
212-682-0435
212-679-4258 Fax
Website: www.caribtourism.com

Founded in 1951 with current membership in 24 countries and territories. Created to develop tourism and integrate it with the development planning of the involved states; and to strengthen the relationship between tourism and development.

Council of Europe (CE)
BP 431 R6
F-67006 Strasbourg Cedex
France
(88) 41 20 00
(88) 41 27 88 Fax
Website: www.coe.fr

Founded in 1949, currently has 21 member governments. Among its eight main activities is one titled «Environment, Regional and Town Planning, Architectural and Archeological Heritage.» Adopted European Charter of the Architectural Heritage in 1975 and in 1985 the «Convention for the Protection of the Architectural Heritage of Europe.»

Europa Nostra
35 Lange Voorhout
NL-2514 EC
The Hague
Netherlands
(70) 35 60 333
(70) 36 17 865 Fax
Website: www.proeuropa.org/europa.html

Also known as the International Federation of Nongovernmental Associations for the Protection of Europe's Cultural and National Heritage. Founded in 1963, it currently has members in 22 countries. Created to awaken the pride of European peoples in their common inheritance of architecture and natural beauty. Organized the Historic Towns Forum. Now merged with International Castles Institute.

European Travel Commission (ETC)
c/o Robert Hollier
2, rue Linois
F-75015 Paris
France
(1) 44 37 37 93
(1) 44 37 38 29

Founded in 1948, currently has members in 27 countries. Created to promote visitor traffic, foster international tourism cooperation in Europe, facilitate exchange of information and undertake travel research. Publishes market research studies and survey reports.

Inter-American Travel Congresses
c/o Organization of American States
International Trade and Tourism Division
1889 F Street, N.W., Third Floor
Washington, D.C. 20006, U.S.A.
202-458-3567
202-458-3560 Fax

Established in 1939 to deal with special technical matters on tourism and develop specific aspects of inter-American cooperation concerning tourism. Currently has 34 members.

International Association of Scientific Experts in Tourism (AIEST)
Varnbülstrasse 19
CH-9000, St. Gallen, Switzerland
(71) 30 25 30
(71) 30 25 36

Founded in 1951 with current membership in 47 countries. Created to promote scientific activity, exchange views and ideas and support the activity of scientific institutes of tourism.

International Automobile Federation (FIA)
8 place de la Concorde
F-75008 Paris
France
(1) 42 65 99 51
(1) 49 24 98 00 Fax

Founded in 1904, currently has affiliated members in 105 countries. Created to develop and organize motor touring in all countries. Organized in a series of Commissions: International Touring, International Traffic, International Technical and International Historic.

International Council on Monuments and Sites (ICOMOS)
49-51 rue de la Federation
75015 Paris
France
(1) 45 67 67 70
(1) 45 66 06 22 Fax
E-mail: icomos@cicrp.jussieu.fr
Website: www.icomos.org

Founded in 1964, the organization has an international committee on cultural tourism.

International Hotel Association (IHA)
251, rue du Faubourg St Martin
75010 Paris
France
(1) 47 00 84 57
(1) 47 00 64 55 Fax

Founded in 1946 with current membership in 140 countries. Created to federate national hotel associations in all countries, study problems affecting international hotel industry and international tourist traffic.

International Touring Alliance (AIT)
c/o Mr. Oliver Mousse
179, ave. Louise
B-1050 Brussels
Belgium
(2) 64 66 230
(2) 73 52 326 Fax

Founded in 1889, currently has members in 86 countries. Created to maintain a world-wide organization upholding the interests of its member associations in all matters concerning international tourism and motoring.

International Union of Architects (UIA)
51 rue Raynouard
F-75016 Paris
France
(1) 45 24 36 88
(1) 45 24 02 78 Fax

Founded in 1948 with current membership in 106 countries. Created to unite the architects of the world. Special work group on «Heritage,» «Cultural and Educational Spaces," and "Sustainable Development."

Organization for Economic Cooperation and Development (OECD)
2 rue Andre Pascal
F-75775 Paris Cedex 16
France
(1) 45 24 82 00
(1) 45 24 85 00 Fax

Founded in 1961 with current membership of 24 governments. Created to help countries promote economic growth, promote sound and harmonious development of the world's economy and improve the lot of developing countries. Created a specialized committee on tourism

Pacific Asia Travel Association (PATA)
1 Montgomery Street, Telesis Tower, Suite 1000
San Francisco, California 94104, U.S.A.
415-986-4646
415-986-3458 Fax
E-mail: PATAHQ@ix.netcom.com

Formed in 1951 to promote travel to countries and islands of the Greater Pacific region. Created a Tourism and Heritage Conservation Committee in 1977.

United Nations Educational, Scientific and Cultural Organization (UNESCO)
World Heritage Centre
7, Place de Fontenoy
75352 Paris 07 SP
France
(1) 45 68 15 71
(1) 40 56 95 70 Fax
Website: www.unesco.org

Oversees the administration of the World Heritage Convention and List. Publisher of *The World Heritage Newsletter.*

World Tourism Organization (WTO)
Calle Capitán Haya, 42
28020 Madrid, Spain
(1) 571 0628
(1) 571 3733 Fax
Website: www.world-tourism.org

Founded 1975 with current membership of 125 countries. Promotes and develops tourism with a view to contributing to economic expansion, international understanding, peace and prosperity. Publishes extensively in area of international tourism statistics, directory, and guidelines.

Cultural Tourism Chronology

A Chronology of Major International Events Related to Cultural Tourism*

(Note: Limited to events related to international cultural tourism.)

1947 International Union of Tourism Organizations (IUTO), predecessor of the World Tourism Organization (WTO), adopts resolutions on the dissemination of knowledge by tourism; and on the development of cultural and popular travel at its 2nd Conference in Paris, France.

1948 IUOTO adopts a resolution on the appreciation of the value of travel to the social and cultural life at its III Conference in Oslo, Norway.

1951 IUOTO adopts a resolution on the promotion of mutual cultural and social appreciation at its VI General Assembly in Athens, Greece.

1957 IUOTO adopts a resolution on African arts and crafts at its XII General Assembly in Washington, D.C.

1960 United Nations Educational, Scientific and Cultural Organization (UNESCO) inaugurates first International Campaign for Nubian Sites in Egypt. Cultural tourism part of overall project planning.

1963 United Nations Conference on Tourism and International Travel, Rome, Italy (August-September). Conference recognizes preservation as an investment in development projects and that cultural tourism has a multiplying economic effect.

1964 UNESCO XIII General Conference adopts resolution calling for study of monuments preservation in relation to the development of tourism and its contribution to a country's economic development. The study's results to be used in helping member states as they undertake actions in this field (October-November).

1965 The Machu Picchu Charter is adopted by a group of experts meeting at Machu Picchu as a result of hotel development proposals.

1966 UNESCO Director-General submits report (72EX/3), «The Preservation of Monuments and Other Cultural Property in Association with the Development of Tourism,» to the UNESCO Executive Board (April).

* Prior to July 1996.

1967 United Nations designates 1967 as «International Tourism Year.»

United Nations Development Program (UNDP) accepts the concept that cultural tourism projects could be financed by them.

Pan American meeting, «The Preservation and Utilization of Monuments and Sites of Artistic and Historical Value,» held in Quito, Ecuador. Adopts report known as the «Quito Standards.»

1969 2nd ICOMOS General Assembly and International Symposium, «Conservation, Preservation, and Enhancement of Monuments and Sites in Connection with the Development of Cultural Tourism,» held in Oxford, United Kingdom (July). Adopts resolution on cultural tourism. Proceedings published in ICOMOS *Monumentum*, Volume VI, 1970.

IUOTO adopts a resolution on the safeguarding of holy places, sites and religious monuments at its XXI General Assembly, Dublin, Ireland.

1970 IUOTO undertakes study for UNESCO to assess the importance of archeological sites and historic monuments as tourist attractions and determine its role in tourism development.

1972 The international treaty, «Convention Concerning the Protection of the World Cultural and Natural Heritage,» adopted by first signatory states.

1973 IUOTO adopts a resolution on the protection of monuments at its XXIII General Assembly in Caracas, Venezuela.

1974 IUOTO holds a seminar in Libreville concerning the role of tourism administration in the protection of the environment and folklore.

1975 Europa Nostra organizes «European Architectural Heritage Year—1975.» International symposium convened in Amsterdam, the Netherlands, in October.

1976 International Council on Monuments and Sites (ICOMOS) Committee on Cultural Tourism sponsors symposium, «Tourism and Humanism — Perspective 2000,» in Brussels, Belgium. It produces «The Charter of Cultural Tourism,» which is signed by 15 participating international tourism-related organizations.

UNESCO and the International Bank for Reconstruction and Development (IBRD-World Bank) jointly sponsor seminar, «The Social and Cultural Impacts of Tourism,» in Washington, D.C. (December). Seminar proceedings published by the World Bank and UNESCO, *Tourism Passport to Development?*, Oxford University Press, 1979.

1978 Organization for Economic Cooperation and Development (OECD) convenes conference, «The Impact of Tourism on the Environment,» in Salzburg, Austria. Proceedings are published in 1980 by OECD.

1979 Pacific Asia Travel Association's (PATA) Committee on Tourism and Heritage Conservation sponsors its first International Conference on Heritage Conservation in Bangkok, Thailand (November). Conference proceedings published by PATA. Subsequent conferences held in Manila, Philippines (1981); Katmandu, Nepal (1983); and Bali, Indonesia (1986).

1980 PATA sponsors first task force with focus on heritage conservation and tourism to Macao. Subsequent numerous task forces sponsored throughout Pacific region.

PATA presents first Heritage Awards to recognize local and national achievements in heritage conservation related to tourism.

WTO adopts «Declaration of Manila on World Tourism» at their general assembly in Manila, the Philippines (September). Declaration includes four major points on cultural tourism.

1982 PATA sponsors first Heritage Training Seminar related to tourism planning and development in Honolulu, Hawaii.

The World Conference on Cultural Policies, organized by UNESCO in Mexico City, Mexico, July 26 - August 6, 1982, adopts Recommendation No. 50 on the protection of objects of cultural tourism and the publication of a world atlas on cultural tourism.

1983 Organization of American States (OAS), the Caribbean Tourism Research and Development Centre and the Caribbean Conservation Association hold seminar on «Cultural Patrimony and the Tourism Product — Toward a Mutually Beneficial Relationship,» in Hastings, Barbados. Seminar proceedings published by the International Trade and Tourism Division, Department of Economic Affairs, OAS, Washington, D.C.

WTO produces study on tourism's contribution to protecting the environment.

1984 International Association of Tourism Experts 1984 Congress has theme of «Tourism and Heritage.»

7th ICOMOS General Assembly adopts the «Charter on Cultural Tourism» in Rostock, German Democratic Republic.

First World Conference on Cultural Parks held in Mesa Verde National Park, Colorado (September). Proceedings published in 1989.

1985 Heritage Trust (United Kingdom) sponsors II International Congress on Architectural Conservation and Town Planning with the theme, «Conservation and Tourism,» Basel, Switzerland (April). Proceedings published in 1986 by Heritage Trust.

The 1st World Congress on Heritage Presentation and Interpretation held in Banff, Alberta, Canada. Congress adopts the «Banff Declaration.»

1988 The 2nd World Congress on Heritage Presentation and Interpretation, with the theme «Preparing for the 90s,» held in Coventry, England, August 4-September 4. Proceedings published by Department of Psychology, University of Surrey, Guildford, Surrey, England, GU2 5H4.

The First Global Conference, Tourism—A Vital Force for Peace, held in Vancouver, B.C., Canada, October 23-27.

1989 The first International Conference on Cultural Tourism, held in Miami, Florida, U.S., April 30-May 3.

First meeting of International Academy for the Study of Tourism, held August in Zakapone, Poland.

1990 Heritage and Tourism: ICOMOS European Conference, held in Canterbury, England, March 1990.

1991 International Symposium on World Heritage Towns organized by the City of Quebec in cooperation with the Government of Canada, the Government of Quebec and UNESCO), June 30-July 4. Adopts "Quebec City Declaration on the preservation of historic urban ensembles in times of change" and forms the World Heritage Towns Network.

Third Global Congress of Heritage Interpretation International: Joining Hands for Quality Tourism—Interpretation, Preservation and the Travel Industry, held in Honolulu, Hawaii, November 3-8.

European Conference on Culture Tourism and Regional Development, held in Leeuwarden, The Netherlands, November 7-8.

European Conference on Culture Tourism and Regional Development, held in Leeuwarden, The Netherlands, November, 7-8. Organized by the Provincial Government of Friesland in cooperation with European Centre for Traditional and Regional Culture, the Christelijke Hogeschool Noord-Nederland, and the European Leisure and Recreation Association.

International Conference on Youth Tourism, New Delhi, India. WTO, November, 18-21.

1992 International Meeting on Quality Tourism, Tel Aviv, Israel, January 23-27.

Tourism and Heritage Conference held in Cairo, Egypt, under the sponsorship of the International Union of Architects Sports, Leisure and Tourism Work Group, February, 1992.

International Workshop on Visitor Carrying Capacity Measurement at Historic Sites and Cities and Wilderness Protected Areas in Developing Countries held in Belize City, Belize, April, 1992.

Tourism at Heritage Sites Conference held in Kathmandu, Nepal, under the sponsorship of the Pacific Asian Travel Association, UNESCO and the International Union for the Conservation of Nature, September 21-23.

Questionnaire, «The World Natural Heritage and Tourism» developed and sent to all natural sites on the World Heritage List under a joint project by UNESCO, United Nations Environmental Program and World Tourism Organization.

International Conference on Cultural Tourism held at Gadjah Mada University in Yogyakarta, Indonesia, on November 24-26, 1992. Adopted the Yogyakarta Declaration on National Cultures and Universal Tourism.

1993 Regional Training Seminar for Cultural Personnel in Asia and the Pacific on theme of Cultural Heritage and Tourism—Preservation and Presentation of Cultural Heritage, held in Tokyo, September 28-October 7. Report available from the Asia/Pacific Cultural Centre for UNESCO, 6, Fukuromachi, Shinjuku-ku, Tokyo 162, Japan.

International Committee for Regional Museums Annual Conference. Theme was Museums and Tourism: the influence of tourism on cultural identity—challenges and possibilities. Held in Cozumel, Mexico, October 24-30.

1994 International Conference on Urban Tourism and City Trips, held in Rotterdam and organized by Erasmus University, Rotterdam, April 28-29.

Second Global Conference of The International Institute for Peace Through Tourism. Theme: Building a Sustainable World Through Tourism. Held in Montreal, Quebec, September 12-16..

1995 World Conference on Sustainable Tourism, held on the island of Lanzarote, Canary Islands, Spain, April 24-29.

Culture and Tourism: Continuity or Change? Yogyakarta, Indonesia, August 23-26.

A PATA Heritage Conference on Tourism: A Force for Conservation of Nature and Culture, held in Laguna Phuket, Phuket, Thailand, September 27-29. Organized by PATA, UNEP, UNESCO.

International Conference on Historic Cities and Sustainable Tourism, organized by ICOMOS/ UK and International Monuments Trust, held in Bath, U.K., October 4-6.

Culture and Tourism: The Challenge for Community Development, organized by European Leisure and Recreation Association, Cesky Krumlov, Czech Republic, October 10-14.

La Carta di Venezia, Trenta Anni Dopo: Incontro Internazionale di Studio (The Venice Charter, 30 Years Later). Part of the celebration of the 30th anniversary of ICOMOS. Held in Naples, November 6-7.

Tourism and Heritage Management: A Profitable Relationship, an international conference held in Aukland, New Zealand, November 21-24.

1996 25-28 March: Third Jerusalem Conference on Heritage, with theme of Making Historic Cities Livable. Organized by Israel ICOMOS.

Case Studies

United Republic of Tanzania, Zanzibar Tourism Development Plan

At the request of the United Republic of Tanzania and the Zanzibar Government, the World Tourism Organization carried out an assistance mission in 1983 to prepare a comprehensive tourism plan for Zanzibar.[1] The objectives of the plan included the development and marketing of tourism, based on the unique historical, cultural and natural attractions of Zanzibar. Among the cultural attractions studied by the mission was Stone Town.

In the following summary of the mission's conclusions and recommendations, it will be seen how the mission was able to draw upon an existing conservation plan in order to make practical suggestions for the restoration and development of Stone Town, not only for tourism, but also for other more general, economic activities.

Stone Town

Stone Town refers to the historic area of Zanzibar town. The district of mostly 19th- and early-20th-century buildings is characterized by a maze-like network of narrow streets and walkways, three to five story "stone" buildings with intricately carved, brass ornamented teak doors and overhanging carved wooden balconies. Interior rooms are narrow with high mangrove pole-beamed ceilings and plastered walls. Most of the 2,500 buildings in Stone Town are used for residences, government offices, and ground-floor retail shops. There are 54 religious buildings, mostly mosques, in Stone Town.

Stone Town is the largest and most impressive of the several Arab style towns built along the East African coast during the centuries of Arab, Persian and Indian trading activities in this part of the world. Because of its uniformly distinctive character, the entire district draws tourists who enjoy wandering along the streets observing the buildings and daily life, as well as visiting specific historic sites.

Despite the intensive use of Stone Town and its appeal to tourists, the district is deteriorating rapidly. Already, several dozen structures have collapsed. General maintenance is required on most of the remaining buildings if they are not to collapse. Unless a comprehensive conservation program for Stone Town is undertaken soon, Zanzibar and East Africa will lose one of its most important and interesting historic and architectural places.

A conservation plan for Stone Town recently has been prepared, whose concepts and development strategy tourism planners strongly endorse. Its approach to conservation maintains the overall historic and architectural character of Stone Town but improves it through renovation of older buildings for modern functions, allowing development of compatibly designed new buildings, improving traffic circulation, upgrading the infrastructure and creating small parks and open spaces. In addition, specific historic structures are slated to be preserved and restored.

[1]For this project, WTO acted as an executing agency of the United Nations Development Program.

The conservation plan also recommends that new and revitalized economic activities be encouraged for Stone Town, including tourism, handicraft and cottage industries such as furniture making. While the town is developed as a tourism center, planners also would like to see beach-oriented resorts develop in other parts of the island and on Pemba. Moreover, careful examination should be made of the consequences of relocating all government functions to the new civic center. It might be better for some government offices to remain in Stone Town, thereby helping to maintain levels of activity and employment. Although it is understood that a Stone Town historic conservation zone has been proposed, it should be adopted soon so that renovation of existing buildings and design of new structures can be done in an architecturally appropriate style. Finally the guided walking tours of Stone Town that are already available should be improved and expanded.

Old Fort (Fort Ngomekongwe):
The Old Fort, built in the Arab style around 1700, occupies a prominent site near Stone Town's waterfront. It would make a suitable cultural center.

House of Wonders (Beit el Ajaib):
The tallest and probably most imposing, aesthetically impressive and best preserved building in Zanzibar is the Beit el Ajaib, built in 1883 as the Sultan's palace. It is recommended that the museum housed in Beit el Ajaib be opened on a regular basis so that both the museum and the palace interior can be appreciated by tourists and residents.

Old Slave Market and Anglican Cathedral:
The site of the infamous slave market in Zanzibar was built over by the Anglican Cathedral in 1873. Both the site and the church are of interest to tourists.

Hamamni Baths:
The Zanzibar government is currently restoring this Persian style bath complex, which is both architecturally and historically interesting. When complete it should be open on a regular basis and the public should be charged an admission fee.

Tippu Tip House:
The home of the notorious slave trader named Tippu Tip, this large house should be preserved because of its historical significance and status as a representative of the Arab architectural style.

Livingstone House:
Located on the outskirts of Zanzibar town, the house was used by David Livingstone in 1866 to organize his last expedition to the mainland interior. In addition to being preserved and restored, this important site should eventually house a museum.

Sri Lanka: Tourism Master Plan

At the invitation of the Sri Lanka government, the World Tourism Organization prepared a tourism master plan in 1991-92. The aim of this study (covering 1992-2001) was to formulate a planned approach to optimize the benefits of the nation's tourism industry. As part of the country's long-term strategic plan, Product Development Programs were formulated, in particular the Ancient Cities of Sri Lanka, noteworthy for the richness of their built heritage. Furthermore, the nation's cultural heritage received special attention in the Five Year Development Program, which formed an integral part of the Master Plan.

As befits a master plan drawn up just prior to the United Nation's Conference on Environment and Development in June 1992, emphasis was placed on putting forward a sustainable tourism development strategy that would respect Sri Lanka's society, traditions and heritage. For this reason, an environmental strategy forms an important part of the master plan.

For the purposes of this case study, interest resides in: a) proposals for access to and infrastructure of the Ancient Cities of Sri Lanka (Anuradhapura, Dambulla, Mihintale, Polonnaruwa and Sigiriya), including tourist facilities and services, buffer zones, interpretation and orientation centers as well as signage and presentation of the monuments themselves; and b) general guidelines developed for cultural heritage sites concerning designation, site planning, environmental impact assessment, visual quality, landscape, circulation, services, lighting, maintenance and management.

Proposals for Ancient Cities Product Development:

- Develop new international-standard hotel accommodations to serve the Ancient Cities of Anuradhapura and Polonnaruwa on sites nearby
- Plan resort facilities and additional standard hotel capacity at Habarana to cater primarily to touring groups making a circuit of the country
- Restrict hotel development in other locations
- Develop a major orientation, interpretation and tourist service complex on the main access road to the sacred city of Anuradhapura
- Develop effective interpretation and orientation centers, incorporating tourist facilities and services at Polonnaruwa, Sigiriya, Mihintale and Dambulla
- Improve signage to and explanation of the monuments of Anuradhapura, Polonnaruwa and Sigiriya
- Improve the presentation of related monuments such as ancient bridges and irrigation canals, thereby broadening the interest of Anuradhapura
- Redesign vehicular traffic patterns and facilities at Anuradhapura and Polonnaruwa and evaluate the introduction of alternative transport at the Ancient Cities
- Protect scenic routes and roads between the main attractions
- Provide infrastructure and facilities to accommodate domestic tourism at the Ancient Cities.

Guidelines for Cultural Heritage Sites

In Sri Lanka primary and secondary heritage sites are major cultural resources and important tourist attractions. They must be protected while conflicts between, for example, cultural and economic values are being resolved. Monuments and sites should be included in a well-structured, integrated planning process involving national, regional and local levels of representation with input from archaeologists, architects, conservators, Ceylon Tourist Board members and other relevant parties.

Site Designation:
there are pressures for development in the vicinity of cultural sites. It is important that until detailed guidelines can be drawn up, primary and secondary cultural sites be "frozen" with no development or new construction permitted within the limits of the archaeological or religious area and designated buffer zone. The sites should be declared National Heritage Parks and have defined boundaries.

Site Planning:
A competent authority should prepare a comprehensive, integrated conservation plan. The plan should

include an interpretation center and museum with artifacts and visual materials related to the site. The museum collections should tell a story based on these objects as well as photographs, site reconstructions, and conjectural building models. Pressure can be relieved at fragile and sensitive areas of the site by development of complementary and compatible attractions elsewhere in the vicinity.

Impact Assessment:
A detailed study of the environmental, sociological and economic resources should be carried out for each site to determine carrying capacity and facilitate future planning of the site. Regular environmental monitoring should also be carried out.

Visual Quality:
Measures for visual protection and enhancement of the site should be addressed. Hills and natural landscape features should be used where possible as a back-drop for the buildings or attractions.

Landscaping:
The designed area should be enhanced using ecologically appropriate trees and vegetation, either that exist today or once did. Landscaping should take account of the need for wind breaks to prevent dust and other hazards from adversely affecting the site.

Circulation:
Pathways and roads within the sites should be simple, compatible and designed for low maintenance. Adequate provision should be made for vehicle parking and circulation routes, and they should be designed and located with minimal negative visual and environmental impact. For large sites, environmentally friendly transport should be encouraged. A secure, well-lit, shaded and gentle landscape will encourage visitors to explore more of the site.

Services:
Care should be taken in the design of toilets, refreshment areas and other services. They should blend in with their environs and be visually unobtrusive. Power and phone lines should be run underground to avoid adverse visual impact. In the event of accident or emergency, there should be an adequate number of telephones distributed within the site. Suitable provision should be made for solid waste collection and removal, as well as waste- and storm-water drainage, collection and re-use.

Lighting:
Careful consideration should be given to flood-lighting to give the monument scale and relate it to the landscape. Planners, however, should adopt a sensitive, nontheatrical approach, incorporating solar power whenever possible as an alternate energy source. General lighting that is compatible with the site should be designed to encourage evening visitation. Sensitive sites such as Dambulla caves require carefully researched and sensitive lighting. Son et lumière presentations also have specialized requirements that need to be considered from the outset.

Maintenance:
Detailed maintenance schedules should be drawn up for each site taking into account the nature and requirements of the monument as well as its support facilities and landscaping.

Management:
Specialist management skills and an appropriate organizational structure are required for the operation and maintenance of cultural sites. Appropriate visitor management systems will increase the capacity of the site and minimize negative impacts.

Poland: Historical Conservation and Tourism Training

In 1988, at the request of the Government of Poland, the World Tourism Organization and the United Nations Development Program organized a study tour for several Polish experts concerned, respectively, with tourism planning and cultural heritage preservation. The study tour had as its objective to assist experts from the Polish city of Cracow and the Wieleczka Salt Mine World Heritage Site to address problems of conservation, upkeep and presentation.

On a study tour to France, Great Britain, Italy and Spain, the Polish experts met their counterparts concerned with heritage conservation and discussed the administrative and institutional structure of those countries, touching on financing mechanisms, cooperation between the tourism administration and the cultural heritage department, and techniques used to conserve, enhance, maintain and present such sites to the public.

The following is an abridged version of the study tour final report, which makes reference to the concluding conference at which the various representatives of the four Western European countries summarized their experiences and approaches to conservation.

This case study highlights the importance of education and training for successful conservation of built heritage sites. It also emphasizes the need to select a conservation strategy in harmony with the administrative and institutional structure of the country in question. Finally, it shows the value of " learning from others" for successful heritage tourism management.

With assistance from WTO, two groups of Polish experts in preservation of cultural heritage, tourism and space planning made field visits to Italy, France, Spain and Great Britain.

In Italy the program was primarily devoted to problems associated with the preservation of cultural heritage. In France and Great Britain, the main topic addressed was the interrelation between tourism and the built environment. The adaptation of historical structures for touristic purposes and tourism planning were the major concerns of the visit to Spain.

The Polish participants saw both positive examples of correlation between tourism and preservation, especially in historical complexes, and instances where the requirements of conservation interfere with tourism. After the study tour, the group presented to the relevant Polish authorities suggestions based on the observations, both positive and negative, made in the four countries. As for Cracow, these suggestions should be useful to the conservation service and tourist organizations. Cracow and its environs--especially the Salt Mine at Wieliczka--need coherent and appropriate planning of correlations between tourism development and preservation of historical sites and buildings.

The study tour to Italy offered the opportunity to learn about the official structure of the state's conservation service and tourism organizations. Special attention was paid to financial and practical aspects as well as to building preservation methods. Italian experts shared with their Polish guests their approaches to conserving wooden ceilings, rafter framing, architectural details, window and door woodwork, floors and stone or brick walls. Members of the group met traditional craftsmen as well as conservation experts.

The visit to France emphasized the working relationship between the conservation community and the tourism sector, not only in Paris but also in other towns. The Polish group learned of the French conservation service and how it is organized. For example, they heard about the General Registry of

Historical Places, which files information concerning all the cultural and historical buildings of France. While traveling in France, the study tour saw renovation work being carried out in the centers of Bordeaux, Carcassone and Nimes, where in addition to being preserved, historical buildings are adapted to meet tourist and recreational demands. The Polish experts studied French methods of financing historical preservation and learned that tourism in France plays a major role in both cultural policy and state finance.

Similarly, in Great Britain, the study group discovered how important tourist development is in Britain's plans for economic revival. Here the role played by private and nongovernmental organizations is greater than in Italy or France.

In Spain, of great interest was the adaptation of historical buildings and complexes for tourist purposes. Magnificent historical buildings serving as tourist accommodations furnished good examples of an effective policy of tourist development and adaptive use of historical structures.

At the end of the study tour, a conference was held in Cracow (May 1989) on the theme, "Renovation of historical towns and tourism." Conference organizers included: the World Tourism Organization based in Madrid, Town Authorities in Cracow, the Ministry of Internal Market, Committee for Young People and Sport Education, Travel Office-Wawel Tourist, Travel Office-Orbis in Cracow.

The conference summarized the 1988 study tour and suggested links between tourism and the renovation of historical towns, buildings and sites. The experience gained on the study tour--mainly in the interface of heritage preservation and tourism--was subsequently put into practice in Poland during the renovation of historical sites in Cracow.

Safranbolu, Turkey

Located on the Black Sea, the Turkish town of Safranbolu is a World Heritage Site. Restoration of monumental structures--the Old Mosque and the Old Baths (1322)--was matched with the adaptation of the 17th and 18th-century merchant houses as guest houses. The monuments were saved but the fabric of the town--the major and minor houses in the town -- were also brought up to World Heritage quality. It was the participation of the residents that made conservation possible and profitable.

There was settlement here in antiquity and Silk Road traffic came through here regularly. By the 18th-century Safranbolu was an important city along the Asia-Europe trade route. The trade created jobs for those making leather goods such as saddles and shoes and blacksmiths prospered. A silk and textile industry flourished.

When the Portuguese, Spanish, Dutch and English ships began sailing around Africa, the town's economy weakened. It was finally crushed by the expansion of railroads and the building of the Suez Canal. Commerce shifted, the rural population moved in. The town stood frozen in time until 1975 when various out-of-towners -- scholars, planners and painters -- joined by helpful government officials, saw tourism as a way to preserve the important unused buildings and provide jobs for the local population.

In 1981, the residents welcomed the idea of tourism but 77 percent of the population had never had contact with a tourist. Yet 77 percent of the population also knew that foreigners bring new money to town. Local custom dictated that a visitor must be housed and fed -- the idea that guests would be asked to pay for room and board was unthinkable.

Today, local customs have been adjusted sufficiently to support a fine hotel in a rehabilitated building, and numerous guest houses operate in the old houses. There are many fine restaurants with total seating for 600. The citizens have formed a foundation to guide, control and manage their growth. Utility lines have been buried, incentives have been offered for residential rehabilitation, and citizens have become critical of poor workmanship.

It was the nearly intact ensemble of an old trade-route city that justified listing it as a World Heritage Site. It was new values, tourism values, that have justified the expense of restoring the monumental buildings. Further, jobs were provided; tourism has employed and satisfied the residents.

Angkor, Cambodia

As Cambodia has opened up, and access to Angkor has again become possible, there is grave danger that tourism could be developed before the conservation programs are in place. This would be a sad, short-term mistake because it is the conservation process that should be the tourism feature at Angkor. The quality of the conservation work determines the quality of the tourism. The quality of life for the residents in the adjacent community of Siem Reap also is a factor in the visitors' experience. Tourism should be limited and for some time expensive, to be sure that the conservation and community plans are created and funded first.

The monuments at Angkor are important and dramatic, but there must be a comprehensive approach to their treatment. It is important also that neither conservation nor tourism divert money away from the urgent social and infrastructure needs of the people of Cambodia.

In this case it has been proposed that visitors pay an annual entry fee of US$150.00 which would go into a privately managed conservation fund dedicated to site repairs and maintenance. This would limit the number of visitors and help assure a sound financial base for development. Once conservation funding and community development plans are in place, then tourism could expand.

Westminster Abbey, London

At Westminster Abbey, the most heavily visited World Heritage Site in the United Kingdom, the Dean and Chapter have so far failed to fake action to prevent the damage caused annually by 3.5 million pair of feet walking over the historic floors. UK/ICOMOS conducted a survey of tourist damage to 44 cathedrals and greater churches in 1991. It revealed a serious level of irreversible damage to medieval floors, the obliteration of inscriptions, for which there is often no record, and systematic theft of and vandalism to monuments. There is severe overcrowding at peak times in the Abbey. Inadequate supervision, particularly in the Royal Chapels, allow many thefts to occur. Tourists have attacked the effigy of King Richard II with an umbrella; stolen the crowns from the effigies of Henry V, Queen Elizabeth I and the Countess of Sussex; stolen fingers, hands and feet from some of the monuments; and have removed fragments of the 13th-century mosaic from the shrine of St. Edward the Confessor. Westminster Abbey is not subject to the controls of the government's Care of Cathedrals Measure. This distressing situation continues.